THE CURRENCY PROBLEM IN CHINA

BY

WEN PIN WEI

AMS PRESS
NEW YORK

COLUMBIA UNIVERSITY
STUDIES IN THE
SOCIAL SCIENCES

144

The Series was formerly known as
Studies in History, Economics and Public Law.

Reprinted with the permission of Columbia University Press
From the edition of 1914, New York
First AMS EDITION published 1968
Manufactured in the United States of America

Library of Congress Catalogue Card Number: 70-76695

AMS PRESS, INC.
NEW YORK, N. Y. 10003

PREFACE

My aim in this study has been not to advocate any particular plan of reform, but rather to present the different phases of the outstanding currency problem in China and to trace the various attempts at reform that have been made since the modern movement for reform in China began. My interest in this subject was first aroused while an undergraduate in Amherst College studying theories of money and banking under Professor John M. Clark. My attention was then called to the unsatisfactory currency conditions in China and this essay may be said to have begun then and there. While by no means an exhaustive treatment of the subject it may, as I hope, serve to familiarize the reader with the nature of the currency problem in its important bearings and likewise with the currency history of China, concerning which there is yet no work covering the whole subject.

Several of my instructors in the Department of Economics in Columbia University and other friends have aided me in the preparation of this work. I take pleasure in acknowledging my indebtedness particularly to Professors Edwin R. A. Seligman and Henry R. Seager for their guidance and help to me in many ways; to Professor Eugene E. Agger, who read the manuscript through and offered many helpful suggestions; and to my friend Professor Jeremiah W. Jenks of New York University, who with great pains made clear to me at different times many difficult points in connection with the problem of currency reform in China. But my greatest obligation is to Professor Wesley C.

Mitchell for the painstaking care with which he has helped me to make this monograph readable and to get it through the press. His many suggestions, as to both matter and form, have without exception been incorporated.

W. P. Wei.

Columbia University, New York City, April 10, 1914.

TABLE OF CONTENTS.

PART I.

HISTORICAL SURVEY.

PAGE

CHAPTER I.

Ancient Money.

CHAPTER II.

Government Paper Money.

PAGE

PART II.

THE PROBLEM OF CURRENCY REFORM.

CHAPTER III.

Currency Conditions in Modern China.

CHAPTER IV.

Currency Reform, 1895-1905.

CHAPTER I

Ancient Money

The classical authority, Ma Tuan Lin,[1] in his *Résumé of Ancient Currencies* asserts that money was in circulation in China as early as the reign of *T'ai-hao* (2953-2839 B. C.) and says further that the money of the dynasties of Hsia (1990-1558 B. C.) and Shang (1558-1050 B. C.) was tri-metallic, namely gold, silver and copper and that there were the *ch'ien*, or the round money, the *pu*, or the bell-shaped money, the *tao*, or the knife-shaped money, and the cowry-shells. Kuan-tze[2] credits Yu, who was founder of the Hsia dynasty, with having made money from metal obtained

[1] Ma Tuan Lin was born in Poyang, in the province of Kiangsi, about 1245 A. D. His *Wen Hsien T'ung K'ao*, or Encyclopædic Researches, published in 1321, is a very extensive historical research work and has, since its appearance, been regarded as the standard book. An historical study of metallic and paper money constitutes vols. viii and ix of this work. Of the paper money he was particularly qualified to treat, as he was an eye-witness of its abuses. There is an authorized continuation of the *Wen Hsien T'ung K'ao*, in which the currency history is brought down to modern times.

The excellent work *On Chinese Currency* by Dr. W. Vissering (elder brother of Dr. G. Vissering, monetary adviser to the Chinese Government), published in English in 1877 at Leiden (both the Congressional Library and the library of Columbia University possess a copy), is a digest of Ma Tuan Lin and covers the history down to the beginning of the Yuan dynasty. The original text in Chinese of the more important passages appears also in Dr. Vissering's work. My citations are from the original Chinese version.

[2] Kuan-tze, the celebrated statesman in the seventh century B. C., in the dukedom of Ch'i (the province of Shantung).

from mines on Mount Li and with distributing it as alms. He also credits Tang, founder of the Shang dynasty, with having extracted metal from the ores of Mount Chuang which he cast into *shu-kin*, or redemption-money, with which to redeem children with whom the poor had been compelled to part on account of the famine and drought. Only these few particulars were handed down, and there is no positive evidence to substantiate these assertions concerning the ancient currency prior to the Chow dynasty. It is generally believed that during these early stages of Chinese history the medium of exchange consisted chiefly of cowry-shells, unwrought metals including gold, and probably any metallic tool of convenient size, and that the *ch'ien*, the *pu*, and the *tao* did not come into use until a much later period.

Chiang T'ai-kung, the celebrated statesman at the time of the establishment of the Chow dynasty, first laid down monetary rules for the coinage of the round money (the cash or *ch'ien*) about the year 1032 B. C. Ma Tuan Lin says, "the gold money unit of the Chow dynasty was the *chin* (or catty) a cubic inch in size and the copper money was round with a square hole in the center." It is also said that the idea of the hole was suggested by the practice of stringing the cowry shells.

The round money did not gain as extensive circulation as the others just spoken of, partly because of the weakness of the central authority and partly for psychological reasons. The *ch'an*, the *pu*, and the *tao*, which we shall presently describe, resembled the implements then in daily use; hence, they were more easily popularized. The round money, on the contrary, had no obvious value in use.

The *ch'an*, or spade-shaped money, the *pu*, or bell-shaped money, and the *tao*, or knife-shaped money, flourished during the feudal era from the seventh till the third century B. C. in practically the whole of what was then China.

Kuan-tze in the dukedom of Ch'i, of which he was the prime minister in the seventh century B. C., gave them regular shapes and fixed weights which must have been an important step toward popularizing their use. These moneys together with the cowry-shells formed the ordinary currency, or the "lower grade (*p'in*) money"; gold, pearls, and precious stones forming the upper two grades (*p'in*) of the circulation.

A FORM OF THE CH'AN-MONEY

OBVERSE

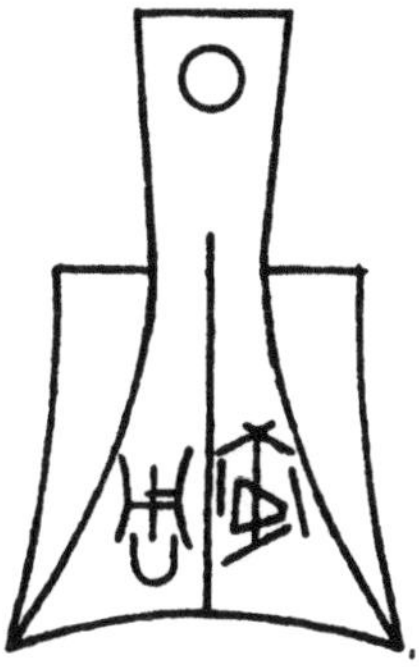

TWO DIFFERENT FORMS OF THE PU-MONEY

OBVERSE OBVERSE

The knife-money of Ch'i is undoubtedly the best known of these ancient moneys, though none of them are today rare. These moneys usually bear legends indicating their places of issue (usually the names of cities) their material, and their "weight-value".[1]

THE CH'I TAO

ROUND MONEY OF EASTERN CHOW PRINCIPALITY
(PROBABLY ABOUT 300 B. C.)

The prince of Ch'in, known by his later title, Shih Huangti, unified the country by gradually subduing all the rival principalities (221 B. C.) His name has always been associated with the building of the Great Wall. He extended the circulation of the round money by prohibiting the use of cowry-shells, pearls, gems, and precious stones as currency. Gold in units of *yi*, 20 taels in weight, was decreed the higher grade (*p'in*) money, and the round money, half-tael in weight, or *pan-liang*, the lower grade (*p'in*), or common currency. It seems that gold in such measures of weight, the *yi* and *chin*, the former 20 taels

[1] *Catalogue of Chinese Coins*, pp. 4-17, on spade-money; pp. 30-212, on the *pu*-money; pp. 213-298, on the knife-money.

The Mint of the United States at Philadelphia has among its collection of Chinese coins samples of the various kinds of money mentioned. A few are also on exhibition in the Metropolitan Museum of Natural History, New York City. The *ts'i-tao* and new *pu*, hereafter described, are also found among the mint collection. So are the Ch'in half-taels.

The weight-value of these moneys is indicated on their face. For instance, the inscriptions on the round money, page 15, indicate that it is "half-tael," and the knife *ts'i-tao*, page 16, 500 (units).

and the latter 16 taels, was used as currency in the early history quite extensively.

THE CH'IN HALF-TAEL ROUND MONEY

OBVERSE

The Han dynasty changed the gold unit of weight from the *yi* of 20 taels to the Chow *catty* of 16 taels. The copper cash, 5 *chu* in weight, (about ⅕ of the tael) was made the standard; but frequent alterations were made in the weight of this unit. The irregular value of the coins in circulation, caused partly by debasement and partly by the presence of counterfeits, led to occasional price disturbances till the reign of Wenti, who, unwilling to enforce the penalty against counterfeiting and seeking at the same time to give the people a convenient currency, decreed free private coinage in 175 B. C. It is recorded that on account of this decree the Prince of Wu, by working the mines of Mount Ch'i obtained large quantities of copper for minting, and that his money had an extensive circulation, whereby he amassed great wealth. Teng Tung, a favorite courtier, was given the mines of the Copper Mountains in the Yentao District, and his coins circulated throughout the empire. In the next reign private coinage was again prohibited.

Wang Mang, while regent, introduced three new varieties of money in addition to the 5 *chu* coin of Han, namely, (1) the "large coin" which was 2 inches in diameter, 12 *chu* in weight, bearing inscriptions meaning "large cash, worth 50"; (2) the *ts'i tao*, worth 500 units the nature of which is not stated; (3) the *tsúo tao*, worth 50 units. When he usurped the throne (7-22 A. D.) the *tao's* and the 5 *chu* coins were suppressed and no fewer than 28 different kinds of money were decreed as the medium of exchange. These 28 kinds of money consisted of gold, silver of two qualities, 4 grades of tortoise shells, 5 grades of cowry-shells, 10 grades of the *pu*, or bell-shaped money, and 6 grades of copper coinage. The shells varied in quality, while the *pu* and the coins varied in size. Just what made him do this it is difficult to tell. The new issues were probably a revival of all the different varieties of money that had existed under the Chow dynasty, the precedents of which Wang Mang was anxious to imitate in every possible way for political reasons.

WANG MANG'S TS'I TAO

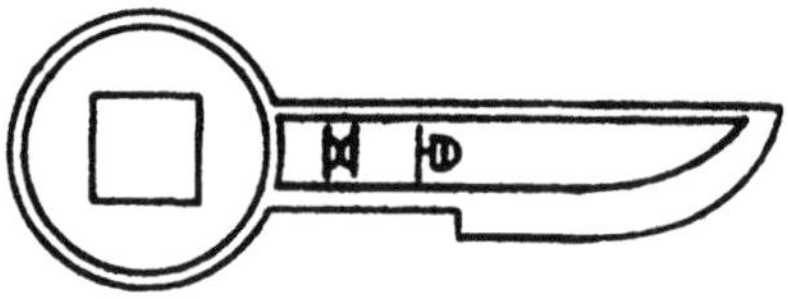

THE NEW PU OF WANG MANG'S REIGN

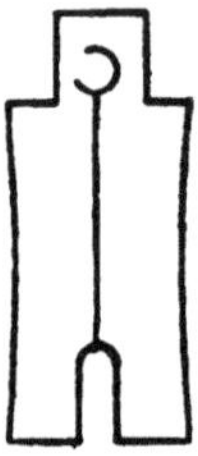

No further development of importance took place in the currency until the time of the establishment of the Tang dynasty. The experiences with the coinage were not encouraging during the years between Han and Tang. Not infrequently efforts were made to abolish the coinage use of metallic money and to return to the use of commodities as the medium of exchange. For instance, under Wenti of Wei in the time of the Three Kingdoms metallic money was decreed abolished (220 A. D.), and measures of grain and rolls of silk were substituted as circulating media. This state of affairs lasted 40 years in Wei until excessive deterioration in these goods led to the restoration of the copper coinage and the use of metallic money again.

After the Tang dynasty had established itself, an attempt was made to standardize the coinage. The Tang coinage regulations were promulgated in the fourth year of Wute (620 A. D.). The coin was fixed at 1/10 of a tael in weight and 8/10 inch in diameter, 1000 coins to weigh 6 catties and 4 taels. Mints were established in several important cities and were put under the supervision of government officials. Counterfeiting was made punishable by confiscation of property and death. The coins which bear the inscription of K'ai Yuan T'ung Pao minted at this time are found to this day among the cash in circulation. One peculiar practice, which was not unfamiliar in mediaeval Europe, was that the right to coin money was granted to three of the emperor's favorites, the princes of Ch'in and Ch'i and Fei-chi.

The policy of the rulers all through these ages appears to have been determined by the principle that coinage was for the convenience of trade and a means of enriching the nation. There is no case on record in which the government tried to make a profit for itself from the issue of copper money. No effort was ever made to coin the precious metals, though both gold and silver were long used as commodity money. Copper on the contrary, was coined, not infrequently in several denominations. In order to have an accurate view of the currency conditions of these early days of history it is necessary to realize that there was a very limited use of the coins. The revenues were always collected in kind, in the agricultural products of the land, and in silk. The country was yet undeveloped and bartering was still the principal method of exchange.

There was marked progress in commerce and trade under the rule of the Tang dynasty, which came into power by putting an end to the long-drawn civil strife. The standardizing of the coinage must have greatly facilitated commerce. However, counterfeit issues soon appeared and it came to pass that the chronicles of coinage under this dynasty were little more than a monotonous repetition of harsh laws against counterfeiting. Owing to the use of a metal which had but slight value, it can be easily imagined that the art of coining must have been simple and inexpensive. This made it possible for false coiners to spring up in large numbers, and coin money by the same process the mints used. Ma Tuan Lin tells us that when the laws which made counterfeiting dangerous were applied effectively on land, the clever coiners transferred their operations to vessels and rafts in the middle of the rivers. This practice led to the issue of an edict in this dynasty to the effect that when there was found above 100 catties of copper and tin on board a vessel it should be confiscated. The art of coining was never improved upon. Dr. Vissering points out the fact that experience elsewhere proves that the most effective means of preventing false coining is to render the mechanical execution of the coin so perfect as to make forgery impossible, and that the best method of coining is not the crude practice of casting the coins in moulds but the process of striking them. But in China coins continued to be cast until the close of the nineteenth century.

It was in the Tang dynasty that paper currency, to which we turn in the following chapter, was invented.

CHAPTER II

GOVERNMENT PAPER MONEY

THE first appearance of paper money was at about the beginning of the ninth century (806 A. D.). It was called, *fei-ch'ien*, or "flying-money."[1] The currency conditions had become intolerable by this time. Not only was the coinage irregular, but the supply of coins was also insufficient, partly because of slow mintage, and partly because of the shortage in the supply of the metals. Even copper and bronze statues and images of Buddha were melted down for metal. To supply the deficiency of copper coins, iron was minted, and in the province of Shu (Szechuan) iron had become practically the only currency. With the development of trade these moneys of copper and iron must have been most inconvenient on account of their weight.

Ma Tuan Lin's description of the appearance of the *fei-ch'ien* is obscure, but enough is given to show its significance. The *fei-ch'ien* was a certificate of deposit issued by government offices in exchange for coins. These certificates were considered so convenient that they soon became part of the circulation. Ma Tuan Lin says that "because the merchants could travel or carry on trade relations in

[1] Ma Tuan Lin tells that in the reign of Wuti (119 B. C.), of the Han dynasty, "pieces of skin of white stags, measuring a square foot and embroidered on the hems, of a nominal value of 400,000" [units not specified], were used among the feudal princes and nobles of the court to represent values. This curious medium of exchange was known as "skin currency". But it can hardly be called currency proper, as it never circulated beyond the few court nobles.

distant places with light equipment, this new currency came to be called 'flying-money'." Fear that it would displace the metallic money led to its suppression. Nothing more is said about it.

Very similar was the *pien-ch'ien,* meaning, as the term denotes, "convenient money" (about 960 A. D.). Like the *fei-ch'ien* it resembled a kind of banking facility offered by the Government to the merchants. It first appeared at the time when the Sung dynasty was established. Merchants coming to the capital were permitted to exchange specie at the Government Treasury for the *pien-ch'ien,* payable in cash on demand at the provincial treasuries. These certificates became current and very popular. Later, issues were made expressly for general circulation. Interesting is the fact that the government managed the *pien-ch'ien* with skill approaching that of the modern banker. A bureau attached to the Treasury was created to issue and redeem the *pien-ch'ien.* These certificates were issued to applicants promptly and measures were taken to secure them against depreciation. For instance, the responsible officials were liable to punishment if these certificates when presented for payment were not promptly redeemed. During the early years of the Sung dynasty until the invention of the *chiao-tze,* according to Ma Tuan Lin, the total amount in actual circulation at any time did not exceed 2,830,000 *kuan* (a *kuan* is nominally 1000 cash).

It was in the province of Shu (Szechuan) that pure paper currency developed into a system. The geographic isolation of this province favored the rise of an independent system. This province had more than once been an independent state, and in almost everything had a little history of its own. After the fall of Wang Mang's government there was a state of confusion all over the country, and as a result Kung-sun Shu proclaimed himself first Governor and later Emperor in this province (25 A. D.). During the eleven years of his reign he put into circulation an iron currency. Thereafter it appears that the people in the province of Shu had used only iron money. The invention of paper currency is told in a striking passage in Ma Tuan Lin's *Résumé of Ancient Currencies.* At the time when Chang Yung, a very noted administrator of this dynasty, was governor of Shu the people were much discontented with the heavy iron coins which they had to use.[1] Sixteen wealthy houses formed a partnership, or "guild," and issued notes, *chiao-tse*, or "exchanges", for circulation. In the course of time these notes practically displaced the specie that had previously been found in circulation and became the currency of Shu. Confidence in the issuers' solvency together with the intolerable conditions produced by the iron currency must have accounted for the popularity of these notes.

But in the course of time, the sixteen wealthy houses got into trouble with their creditors and the people discovered that the notes did not actually represent specie. There were lawsuits. After much deliberation the *chiao-tse* was declared inconvertible paper currency, and the government took over the right of issue from the private concern, and vested it in a government *chiao-tse* office established in Yi-chow, the capital city of the province.

Later, the central government began to issue *chiao-tse* currency notes on its own account. By the first year of Tien-sheng (1032) the issues outstanding at a given date were about 1,250,000 kuan (or 1,256,340 kuan exactly) and the government kept a specie reserve of 360,000 kuan.

[1] Of the iron money in Shu, Lu Tung-lai says (*Ma Tuan Lin*, vol. ix) that it weighed 25 catties per 1000 pieces for the large ones and 10 catties for 1000 small ones, and that it was the only currency at the time when *chiao-tse* was invented.

The amount of issue seems to have been restricted to the actual demand for the paper currency and the paper was protected carefully against depreciation.

But the danger of depreciation through excessive issue was there. When the prolonged struggle with the Tartars exhausted the government's resources, the government resorted to the issue of paper currency as a means of raising revenue. Never before, as far as is known, had a Chinese government attempted to secure a financial gain for itself from the authority over the monetary system. Excessive issue led to the depreciation of the paper currency and arbitrary means were devised to check the decline and even to restore the paper to its metallic value. Thus it was made a rule that when among the people business was transacted to the amount of 10,000 cash, or 10 kuan, and upwards, half of this sum must be paid in specie and the other half in the paper currency. It was thought that by this means it would be difficult for the people to ascertain and compare the fluctuations in the value of the paper, and that the latter value would be brought back to equivalence with that of the metallic money. It was soon found that all these artificial methods were futile to check depreciation caused by over-issue. Ma Tuan Lin states that there was in circulation, at the time when the Sung seat of government was moved southward, twenty times the original amount fixed upon as the actual requirements of commerce, and that the *chiao-tze* fell to about ten per cent of its par value. The weakened political power of the Sung government, in the face of repeated defeats by the Chin Tartars, helped to lessen the credit of the paper money.

It is not necessary to go into all the details of the history of the paper currency, which lasted from this time on to the Ming dynasty. All the experiences in America and France with inconvertible paper currency, the Chinese people had gone through centuries ago. In the monetary history of the country the interesting fact cannot escape attention that the government paper currency marked the transition from the ancient régime of copper and iron to the modern régime of silver and copper. The general features of the paper issues of the subsequent reigns and dynasties, under one name or another, may now be noticed.

The Southern Sung Paper Currency and the Chin Ch'ao

From the reign of Kao-tsung, 1130, till the conquest of the whole country by the Mongols, China was separated into two halves, the Southern Sung dynasty holding the southern half and the Chin Tartars ruling over the northern half. They were constantly at war with each other. Both issued inconvertible paper currency for purposes of revenue.

I. *The Southern Sung Dynasty.* In 1131 the *kuan-tze* or "frontier-bills" were issued through payment of the troops stationed on the frontiers. These bills were forced into circulation and were heavily discounted. There were likewise *tea-notes, grain-notes* and *silk-notes,* exchangeable for so much tea, *etc.*, as was expressed on the note. The failure of the *kuan-tze* led to a reorganization of the paper currency and to a new variety with new devices. The *hui-tze,* one of the best known of the government paper currencies, was invented in 1159.

The *hui-tze* replaced whatever paper there was then in circulation. It was in four denominations, 500, 300, 200 cash and the usual one-kuan note. Public dues were payable in these notes at par value. The government financiers could not get away from the erroneous notion that the disappearance of the metallic currency was the *cause* of the depreciation of the government paper; so efforts were again made to regulate the methods of making payments. It was accordingly decreed that in the receipt of public dues and in public disbursements one-half must be paid in specie and the other half in paper, except in those places remote from the main waterways where taxes and tributes might all be receivable in the *hui-tse*. The application of this decree was extended to all business transactions.

The government manufactured the paper for the currency notes. These notes were stamped with the Treasury seal before they were put into circulation. The Treasury seal gave the notes the character of fiat money. The issue of paper currency was a government monopoly and forging notes was punishable according to the law of forging state documents.

When the paper currency became excessive, occasional conversions were made. The method of triennial redemption of old notes by a new series was followed. Aside from the *hui-tse* just described there were several local issues under different names and devices.

The Chuan *yin*, or Szechuan paper notes, almost totally displaced the metallic circulation and in 1161 reached the enormous sum of 41,470,000 kuan. The total amount of iron coins was said to be no more than 700,000 kuan. In Kia-ting's reign, 1208, the Chuan *yin* was worth in this province 40 per cent of its par value in iron money, while outside this province, where copper money was in circulation, the paper currency was worth 17 per cent of its par value.

Towards the close of the Southern Sung dynasty when the finances of the state were in dire straits the paper currency on account of excessive issue was in a state of rapid decline. When the value of the paper became low, a greater quantity had to be issued and forced into circulation in order to get the needed amount of supplies. In 1263 a last effort was made to revive the paper currency and the *kuan-tse* was again resorted to. It was issued in exchange for the *hui-tse*.

There were both silver and copper *kuan-tse*. But meanwhile the Mongols had already conquered the Chin dominions and in 1279 the Southern Sung dynasty came to an end.

II. *The Chin Tartars.* The Chin Tartars in Northern China followed the Sung paper-currency system. The Chin paper currency, likewise inconvertible, was called *ch'ao,* a name subsequently adopted to denote both government paper currency and banknotes quite indiscriminately. The Chin *ch'ao* was of many denominations, ten in number, namely, 10,000, 5000, 3000, 2000, and 1000 cash notes " for use in large payments ", and 700, 500, 300, 200, 100 cash notes " for use in small payments ", or, in other words, as subsidiary currency. The *ch'ao* notes were redeemable in a new series once in every seven years, at the charge of 15 cash per note. The system in the Chin dominions was more centralized than in the Southern Sung Empire. Both the *ch'ao* and the paper currency of Southern Sung were repudiated when the Mongols conquered and united China under the new dynasty, the Yuan dynasty.

The Yuan Dynasty Paper Currency

The Yuan dynasty lasted 88 years (1279-1367). The *pao ch'ao,* or " precious notes ", were decreed the sole legal currency in which all prices must be fixed, in the third year of Kublai Khan, 1260, which was before the Mongols had completed their conquest of the Chinese Empire. Exchange offices were established in all commercial centres, where worn-out notes were redeemed in new ones at an arbitrary charge, usually three per cent of the par value of the note. Taxes and dues were payable in these notes. The paper currency issued in this period was known as the series of Chungtung and the notes were in ten denominations ranging from 10 to 2000 cash.

A very interesting contemporary account of the paper currency given by Marco Polo may be quoted.[1]

With regard to the money of Kambulu,[2] the great Khan may be called a perfect alchemist, for he makes it himself. He orders to collect the bark of a certain tree, whose leaves are eaten by the worms that spin silk. The thin rind between the bark and the interior wood is taken, and from it cards are formed like those of paper, all black. He then causes them to be cut into pieces, and each is declared worth respectively half a liver, a whole, a silver grosso Venice, and so on to the value of 10 bezants. All these cards are stamped with his seal, and so many are fabricated that they would buy all the treasures in the world. He makes all his payments in them, and circulates them through the kingdoms and provinces over which he holds dominion; and none dares to refuse them under pain of death. All the nations under his sway receive and pay this money for their merchandise, gold, silver, and precious stones, and whatever they transport, buy or sell. The merchants often bring to him goods worth 400,000 bezants, and he pays them all in these cards, which they willingly accept, because they can make purchases with them throughout the whole Empire. He frequently commands those who have gold, silver, clothes of silk and gold, or other precious commodities, to bring them to him. Then he calls 12 men skillful in these matters, and commands them to look at these articles and fix their price. Whatever they name is paid in these cards, which the merchant cordially receives. In this manner the great sire possesses all the gold, silver, pearls and precious stones in his dominions. When any of the cards are torn or spoiled, the owner carries them to the place whence they were issued and receives fresh ones, with a reduction of 3 per cent. If a man wishes gold or silver to make plate, girdles, or other ornaments, he goes to the office, carrying a sufficient number of cards, and gives them in pay-

[1] Murray's *Polo*, p. 137. Also Sir Henry Yule's *Polo*, bk. ii, chap. 24.

[2] *Kambulu*, namely, Peking.

ment for the quantity which he requires. This is the reason why the Khan has more treasure than any other lord in the world; nay, all the princes in the world together have not an equal amount.

Besides this passage Marco Polo frequently mentions the circulation of the *ch'ao* in those places where commerce was flourishing.

In 1284 a new series, called *pao ch'ao* of Chihyuan, was issued. These new notes were exchangeable for those of the Chungtung variety at the rate of 1 to 5, in other words, one note of the new series was to exchange for five of the previous series of equal nominal value. Sir Henry Yule estimates that during the 34 years when Kublai reigned the lowest issue was 228,960 kuan in 1269 and the highest was 50,002,500 kuan in 1290, while the total amount during the 34 years reached the enormous sum of 249,654,290 kuan.[1]

The third and last series issued by the Mongols was known as the *pao ch'ao* of Chihta (1310). These were silver notes exchangeable for those of the Chihyuan series at the rate of one to five and for those of the Chungtung series, 1 to 25. One tael silver and one kuan cash (nominally 1000) were used as nominally equivalent in value.

The Mongol Conquest opened the country to extensive commercial relations with other parts of the Asiatic continent and the tea and silk trades brought into the country a steady importation of silver. The use of silver as currency was rapidly extended under this dynasty. The familiar

[1] Yule, *op. cit.*, p. 427, footnote. The currency notes have often been called banknotes. To me this seems to be a misnomer, for they are inconvertible paper money pure and simple. Between the two kinds of credit money there is a fundamental difference. Samples of the Ming *ch'ao* are not rare to-day. There is one reproduced in Yule's *Polo*. Vissering's book also contains a reproduction.

units of weight, the *liang*, or tael, and the *ting*,[1] were used as the silver currency units. With the downfall of the Yuan dynasty and the subsequent repudiation, the régime of paper currency was practically closed, though the Ming rulers never completely gave it up.

The Ming Dynasty Paper Currency

Ming Tai-tsu sought to re-establish the paper currency and in 1367 decreed that the coins minted by the government mints and the paper currency, the Ming *ch'ao*, were to circulate side by side at par and no discrimination was to be shown in favor of one as against the other, but both were to be legal money. But no sooner were the new *ch'ao* notes issued than they were heavily discounted and soon they were worth only 5 per cent of their nominal value. In spite of all artificial regulations the efforts to maintain their value were unsuccessful. Silver was looked upon with suspicion and was regarded as the cause of the failure of the paper currency, and accordingly Ming Tai-tsu issued a decree prohibiting the use of silver as currency. Repeated abuses of the credit of the government at last destroyed all popular confidence in the government's good faith. Though many further attempts were made to re-establish the paper circulation in the subsequent reigns of this dynasty popular suspicion that the same course of depreciation followed by repudiation might be the outcome was sufficient to render all those efforts futile.

The Manchu, or Ch'ing dynasty was established in 1644 and during the first few years of Shun-chih's reign it appears that an attempt was again made to issue paper currency in very much the same way as it had been issued in the previous dynasties. The chronicles show that about

[1] A *ting* is nominally 50 taels.

120,000 kuan per annum was issued for some time but this practice was soon given up. Paper-currency issues were subsequently condemned by the Manchu House and in 1815 during the Emperor Kia-ching's reign. Ts'ai Chih-ting, one of the Ministers of State, was severely rebuked for advocating its revival. However the past experiences were easily forgotten in time of financial straits and during the Tai Ping Rebellion paper money was again resorted to as a means of raising revenue. Currency notes in the reign of Hsien-feng of 1, 3, 5, 10, and 50 teals silver and of 500, 1000, 1500 and 2000 cash (copper) were forced into circulation (1856). They rapidly depreciated and were soon worth next to nothing. As before the government repudiated these notes.

The ancient records are fragmentary and, in many places, vague and obscure in their meaning. In the above general survey practically all that is of any importance about the metallic and paper currencies of the past is included.

CHAPTER III

Currency Conditions in Modern China

The currency of modern China cannot, properly speaking, be called a system. It is composed of a number of systems. There is the cash coinage; the currency of silver bullion based on the tael unit; silver coins, the dollars of foreign as well as of provincial mintage; and finally there are the minor silver coins, fractional parts of the dollar circulating independently of the unit and with no limitations upon their legal-tender quality. We may, however, regard the currency as on a bimetallic basis with the copper cash and the silver tael as the units. This must not be mistaken for real bimetallism. Bimetallism in the sense in which it is understood in the West requires free coinage of two metals (gold and silver) both of which are legal tender, with a *fixed ratio* between the units of coinage. The two metals in the Chinese currency, on the contrary, are independent of each other and circulate without a fixed exchange-ratio between them. The cash is a standard coin; the tael an uncoined unit of weight. There is a tradition that the cash was intended to be in value the equivalent of one-thousandth of a silver tael, but such a notion has at no time any practical validity since the exchange between the two units depends generally upon their values as metals in the market.

I. *The Cash.* According to one authority the standard weight of this coin should be 57 grains of the metal of which it is made—copper and as much spelter or zinc (sometimes lead) as the copper will take up.[1] According to another writer [2] the cash is described as

a circular coin rather more than an inch in diameter with a square hole in the middle for the convenience of stringing. It should consist of an alloy of copper, 50%; zinc, 41½; lead, 6½; tin, 2; or of equal parts of copper and zinc. Each piece should weigh 58 grains troy, or 3.78 grams; but these standards of composition and weight are not free from counterfeiting and the cash in circulation would not measure up to them generally.

Of the issues of the Manchu dynasty, those of the reigns of Shun-chih (1644-1661), K'ang-hsi (1661-1721) and Yung-cheng (1721-1735), as they are now found in actual circulation, are larger and of better quality than those of Ch'ien-lung (1735-1795), Chia-ch'ing (1795-1820) and Tao-kuang (1820-1850), all of which are superior to the issues of the later reigns both in substance and in size. The issues of previous dynasties are found in circulation in considerable numbers, mostly defaced and much worn. The K'ai Yuan coins issued in the Tang dynasty are by no means rare, and have formed part of the every-day currency of the people for twelve centuries. Those of the Tai Ping rebel government are not at all discriminated against. Counterfeiting practices are so common that they have been one of the chief causes of frequent price inflations in local markets and counterfeit coins are usually accepted without question.

The following three causes may therefore account for the lack of uniformity in weight and in size of the cash coins:

First. Concurrent circulation of issues of many reigns

[1] Dr. G. Morrison, in *The London Times Fin. and Com. Supplement*, Mar. 13, 1905.

[2] T. Jernigan, *China's Business Methods*, p. 80.

of the Manchu dynasty with the survivals of issues of preceding centuries.

Second. The crude method of coining which rendered uinformity impossible, particularly when the cash mints were not under the control and management of one central authority.

Third. The circulating of many counterfeit coins. Until recently, the cash has always been cast in moulds which made counterfeiting quite easy.

In ordinary transactions no discrimination is made on account of these differences, and even the counterfeit coins, unless they reach a considerable proportion of the circulation, pass comfortably as regular coins. For these reasons the cash may be considered a coin of universal acceptability. Except in the trade centres it is the only currency.

The Peking cash currency. During the second half of the last century Peking had a currency of its own which was not demonetized until a few years ago (1907) and which deserves special mention. This consisted of the debased and depreciated 10-cash pieces.

The Peking 10-cash coin had a little history of its own. It dated back to the time of the Tai Ping Rebellion when the supply of copper from Yunnan was cut off. The currency notes mentioned in the previous chapter were issued at this time (1856) in Hsien-feng's reign. Partly for purposes of raising money and partly in order "to continue the manufacture of cash" the Government issued many token coins of 5, 10, 50, 500 and 1,000 cash pieces. Iron coins were also minted. These coins never gained a circulation outside Peking, though it is said that some provincial mints also made them. These token coins caused considerable business disturbances in the capital. All of them became depreciated and soon all but the 10-cash pieces disappeared. The latter became the cash currency of Peking, the regular coins having meanwhile been displaced by the depreciated coins. The 10-cash piece circulated at the depreciated valuation of 2-cash. The coinage of multiples of the cash had frequently been resorted to in previous dynasties. As will presently appear, the Peking cash was replaced by the new copper coinage in 1907.

The tiao. Cash currency is reckoned in terms of *tiao,* of nominally 1,000 coins. Through an age-long practice of discounting and rediscounting the *tiao* has come to be quite different from what it had been meant to be. As it is used to-day the *tiao* varies widely among the different districts. For instance, it is 490 coins in Tientsin (one counting as two, and 49 coins passing as 100). In Lanchow and all the eastern section of the country the *tiao* represents from 160 to 163 coins, 16 usually passing as 100. In Peking when the depreciated cash currency was in use 49 to 50 passed as 1,000 (one coin counting as two and the cash being the depreciated 10-cash coins). In Yunnan city in southwestern China the same confusion of the cash currency prevails. In Yunnan city the *tiao* consists of 620 coins, 62 here passing as a nominal 100, while outside the city the *tiao* represents 980 coins, 98 passing as a nominal 100. Just what this involves may be seen from the following illustration:[1]

This part of Hupei province has long been distinguished for its variety of rates of exchange. A nominal 100 cash has for a long time been 97 in actual cash at Wusueh, 98 at Lungping, 97 or 98 in different classes of transactions at Hsiangkuo, 90 miles away, and 99 at Chi-chow, the same distance away in another direction. To complicate matters, the only cash bills which are popular are issued by a Wusueh bank and are current in all these towns, but not at face value. At Wusueh a bill equals 1000 cash (one *tiao*). At Lungping one has to give 10 cash and a bill for 1000, and at Chi-chow one must add 20 cash to the bill.

[1] *North China Daily News,* May 11, 1906.

This particular district is not exceptional but rather typical of the local currency conditions. Much more might be said of the *tiao*, but the preceding suffices to show that one is likely to commit all kinds of miscalculations in converting the currency of one locality into that of another. That such inconvenience hinders the proper development of trade is obvious

II. *The Silver Currency*. The establishment of the silver currency has been gradual, even to-day in the interior regions cash is almost the sole currency. Silver was first introduced as currency in commerce during the paper currency régime, though without the sanction of the government. It is impossible to determine the date of this innovation even approximately. History tells us that Ming Tai-tsu, 1367, in order to maintain the paper currency attempted to prohibit the use of silver currency. Nevertheless, silver came into extensive use as currency under the Ming dynasty, and since the establishment of the Manchu dynasty most large transactions and Treasury operations have been conducted in silver.

A great deal of the silver stock in China came from foreign commerce. Direct foreign trade with the Western countries began at Canton in 1516, first with the Portuguese. During the early years, the tea and silk trades brought into China a steady importation of silver. Mr. H. B. Morse estimated that the imports of goods never equaled the exports of tea and silk during the eighteenth century; indeed, that such imports never amounted to one-fifth of the exports. The balance was always paid in silver. He estimated that the total importation of silver into China from 1700 to 1830 could not be less than $500,000,000.[1] With the ex-

[1] Statistical Secretary of the Chinese Maritime Customs. *China and the Far East*, Clark Univ. Lectures, 1910, pp. 96-97.

pansion of the opium trade the balance began to be paid in opium. In 1837, shortly before the Opium War, opium constituted 57 per cent of the total value of the imports at Canton.[1] Later in the nineteenth century, when conditions differed from previous times, the importation of silver continued on a large scale. Sir Rober Giffen[2] gave some interesting facts about the movement of the precious metals between China and other nations before the British "Royal Commission ou Gold and Silver" in 1886. After an examination into the statistics of the chief countries with which China trades, he found that China exported on balance to the chief commercial countries it trades with every year from about £1,000,000 to £2,000,000 sterling of gold. He found that the export of gold was a little over £1,000,000 on the average for the years 1864 to 1886. As to the silver, he found that concurrently with the export of gold China was importing silver and that there was an excess of imports over exports of silver. This excess was £5,300,000 in 1877, the largest balance of the twenty-seven years he studied.[3] From this statistical evidence it appears that China has been a regular silver-importing country and has exported a considerable amount of her gold.

The tael unit. The silver currency unit is the *tael*, decimally divided into mace, candareens, *etc.* The tael in the Chinese system is a measure of weight as well as a money of account. Through lack of governmental regulation, the tael has come to be in the course of time very irregular in weight. Again, the purity of the silver bullion is liable to variation. Thus commercial usages have come to recognize

[1] *China and the Far East*, Clark Univ. Lectures, 1910, p. 100.

[2] Royal Com. on Gold and Silver, *Minutes of Evidence*, p. 21.

[3] *Ibid.*, p. 29 and pp. 314-15. Figures for 1858-85.

several degrees of fineness in the bullion in every important market. The weighing and testing of the bullion involve not only loss of time but danger of inaccuracy. Of course, modern nations in the West have got over this difficulty by means of coinage. The coins are minted by the Government and each contains a fixed amount of metal of an invariable degree of fineness. All the trouble of the use of bullion is thus done away with. The Chinese Government has never, until recent years, attempted to coin silver.

Nor has any attempt been made until recently to define the exact weight of the tael and to introduce uniformity in the standard by government action. The Treasury has one standard, the Ku'p'ing tael. Each city or commercial guild has practically one for its own use, and when duties on imports were to be levied according to commercial treaties a Customs tael, or Haikuan tael, different from all the rest, was adopted as a money of account. This lack of uniformity in the weight and value of the tael is by no means exceptional among Chinese measures. The units of weight, of capacity, and length all vary from use to use and from place to place. The catty may be taken as an example. The catty (16 taels in weight) weighs exactly one and one-third pounds on the scales of the Maritime Customs. In Shanghai the following measures are found: in foreign dealings the catty is 20.4 oz.; the regular "guild" catty is 19.7 oz.; the catty for rice for the grain tribute is 20.6 oz.; in the sale of oil it is 23.2 oz.; in the sale of sugar it is 27.25 oz.[1] As a similar state of affairs prevails in almost all of the centres of trade, the variations of this one measure of weight can be imagined.

The following account showing the nature of the silver tael currency in the city of Chungking is taken from the

[1] *London Times*, June 5, 1905.

Times,[1] and is true more or less of all the trade centres of the country:

Here (in Chungking) the standard weight of the tael for silver transactions is 543.7 grains, and this is the standard for all transactions in which the scale is not specified. Usually, however, a modification is provided for, depending in some cases upon the place from which the merchant comes or with which he trades, and in others upon the goods in which he deals. A merchant coming from Kweichow, or trading with that place, will probably, but not certainly, use a scale on which the tael weighs 537.2 grains; a merchant from Kwei-fu, a town on the Yangtze, a hundred miles from Chungking, will buy and sell with a tael of 550.7 grains; and between these two extremes are at least ten topical [*sic*] weights of tael all "current" at Chungking. In addition to these twelve topical "currencies" there are others connected with commodities. One of the most important products of Szechuan is salt, and dealings in this are settled by a tael of 544.5 grains, unless it is salt from the Tze-liu well, in which case the standard is 545.7 grains. A transaction in cotton cloth is settled with a tael of 543.1 grains, but for cotton yarn the tael is 544.1, and for raw cotton the tael is 536.0 grains.

This seems confusion, but we are not yet at the end. Up to this point we have dealt only with the weight of the scale, but now comes in the question of the fineness of the silver with which payment is made. At Chungking three qualities of silver are in common use—"fine silver" 1000 fine current throughout the Empire, "old silver" about 995 fine, and "trade silver" between 960 and 970 fine; and payment may be stipulated in any one of these three qualities. Taking the score of current tael weights in combination with the three grades of silver, we have at least 60 currencies in this one town.

The three principal taels are the K'up'ing, or Treasury

[1] *London Times*, March 13, 1905. *Cf.* H. B. Morse, *The Trade and Administration of the Chinese Empire* (1907), p. 145.

tael, the Haikuan, or Customs tael, and the Shanghai tael, which is the tael for international trade.

The K'up'ing tael. The Board of Revenue tael contains 575.8 grains of silver, 1000 fine,[1] and on this basis 100 HK. taels = 101.642335 KP. taels. The K'up'ing tael compared with the Shanghai tael is in the ratio of 100 K'up'ing to 109.60 Shanghai taels.[2]

The Haikuan tael. As the term denotes, this is the tael used in the payment of tariff duties fixed in 1842. It is 1000 fine, containing 583.3 grains; but it is a purely theoretical unit, adopted as a money of account. Though the duties are calculated in this unit, they are paid in the locally current tael to a bank designated as a "customs bank", at a rate of conversion officially fixed upon. Thus at the Shanghai port, for every 100 HK. taels the merchant pays 111.40 Shanghai taels;[3] at Ningpo at the rate of 1.0583 Chiang-ping

[1] The Kuping fine silver is commercially 1000 fine. It is 987-985 chemically pure silver.

Mr. H. B. Morse, who is perhaps the best known authority on the tael currency system, treats quite extensively in his writings cited here the weight and value of the different kinds of tael currencies. The rate of conversion of the HK. tael into the Shanghai tael is obtained in this manner:

100 HK. taels = 111.40 Shanghai taels:

weight on local scale		100. 0.0.0
add for difference in weight		2. 8.0.0
add for touch		6. 1.6.8
add for melting expenses		0. 2.0.4
		109. 1.7.2
Divide by the "Shanghai Convention" an understanding by which 98 taels settle a liability of 100 taels	0.98	
		111.40

[2] Morse, *The Trade and International Relations of the Chinese Empire* (1908), p. 160.

[3] Dr. J. C. Ferguson, "The Chinese Banking System in Shanghai," *N. C. Daily Herald*, pp. 473-498, March 2, 1906.

tael to 1 HK. tael;[1] at Tientsin, 105 Hangping taels for every 100 HK. taels;[2] and so on.

The Shanghai tael. This is the standard of international exchange for the trade of Northern China and the Yangtze valley. The par of exchange is found from this tael and the London price of bar silver and is given by Mr. Morse as follows: In the Shanghai tael are contained 524.93 grains of fine silver. An ounce of British standard (925) silver contains 444 grains of fine silver. The par of silver exchange is found by dividing the London price by 0.864.[3]

A great deal more might be said about the tael currency system, but what has been given suffices to show the variableness of this monetary unit and the causes of the variations. The result of employing uncoined silver currency with such an imaginary currency unit has been most unsatisfactory. No other single factor has been so great a hindrance to the development of the internal commerce of the country and trade relations with the outer world. Higgling not only about the quantity but also about the quality of silver forms an essential part of legitimate business, and when a merchant trades with distant places careful deductions and fine calculations about the currency are necessary in order to prevent making mistakes. Furthermore, the rate of exchange between this silver currency and the cash currency is a fluctuating one, there being no fixity between these two standards. Under these circumstances the business of money-changing has become a very lucrative trade. The money-changers perform the useful function of converting one currency into another, in order that purchases can be made with the money that is "current" in such pur-

[1] Commissioner E. B. Drew to Sir Robert Hart (1878), *Report of the Int. Exc. Comm.*, 1904, p. 216.

[2] Detring to Hart (1878), *ibid.*, p. 211.

[3] H. B. Morse, *op. cit.*, p. 161.

chases. Dr. Morrison, in the series of articles already referred to, sums up the situation by declaring that "Germany a century ago was a paradise of money changers, with its countless coinages each circulating in its own principality; but that was simplicity itself compared with China."[1] To those who are conversant with the intricacies of the Chinese currency this is but a mild statement of facts.

III. *Foreign Dollars.* Foreign dollars found their way into China in the course of centuries of coast trade. The history of the dollar is a very interesting one. It is said that the Portuguese and the Spanairds brought dollars into China as early as the seventeenth century. These coins soon gained popularity, and later the East India Company imported dollars with which they bought tea and silk.[2] The early trade relations were carried on almost exclusively through Canton city, and that port by an edict issued in 1757 was made the sole trading-post. It remained so until after the Opium War.

The coin that gained the greatest popularity in the early foreign trade was the carolus dollar of the reign of Charles IV (1788-1808) of Spain. Speaking of the American trade in the early nineteenth century, Mr. H. B. Morse says that American products were shipped to Europe, and there sold; the proceeds in Spanish dollars were then sent back to America for transmission to China. Or the ship might be engaged for a time in the carrying trade between the Euro-

[1] David A. Wells, speaking of the monetary system of Germany before 1873, says that it consisted of 17 varieties of gold money; 66 different coins of silver, possessing full legal-tender powers and constituting (1870) 65.7 per cent of the entire circulation; 46 kinds of notes issued by 35 different banks, besides paper money of various kinds to the extent of 7.5 per cent of the circulation. *Recent Economic Changes*, p. 226.

[2] *China Review*, vol. iii, p. 2, year 1874-75.

pean ports, which was very profitable to neutrals during the Napoleonic wars, until she had accumulated a sufficient sum in Spanish dollars with which she then sailed for Canton. Tea and silk were shipped back in exchange for these coins.[1] In another place the same author says that during these years 60 per cent of the total value of the trade with the United States was in Spanish dollars.[2]

"Imitation dollars" were made at Canton by individuals with permission of the officials. It is said that the Provincial Treasurer once ordered the silversmiths to make dollar pieces "like those made by the foreigners" in Ch'ien-lung's reign (1735-1795). This order caused trouble. Profit led the silversmiths to use more alloy until they got to mixing five parts of alloy with eight parts silver. The result was that these coins soon depreciated in the market and subsequently orders were issued to prohibit private coining. But it seems that the order was not effective.[3]

There were various other things which tended to destroy popular confidence in the foreign dollars after they had gained circulation to a considerable extent. Many coins were debased by fraud. For instance, it is said that these coins were filed or pared all around the edge to the extent of a mace or so each, and these "sweated dollars" were mixed with the sound ones which would then pass off on unwary people; and that sometimes the coiners would drill a small hole in the edge of the dollar and scoop out a good deal of the interior silver, replacing it with lead and neatly soldering a bit of silver over the hole.[4] The debasement of the sound coins and the circulation of "imitation dollars"

[1] H. B. Morse, *op. cit.*, p. 84.

[2] *Ibid.*, p. 93.

[3] *China Review*, vol. iii, p. 8.

[4] *Ibid.*, p. 4.

led the business men to adopt precautionary measures; hence we have what are commonly called the "chopped dolars".

The "chopped dollar" resulted from over-precaution. The merchant into whose hands the foreign coins came, having lost his confidence in them, would chop them with an impressed ideagram, usually about one-eighth of an inch square, thereby giving them his guarantee of genuineness. When this was repeated by each succeeding banker the coins became defaced and resembled a sort of disc. The "chopped dollars" were in general circulation at Canton.

Attempts to coin silver dollars seem to have been made in other places by local authorities. It is said that an attempt was made to coin the silver tael currency at Shanghai about 1856. A coinage of dollar pieces was also tried in the provinces of Fuchien and Formosa about 1835 to pay the troops. One specimen bears an inscription stating that it was "pure silver for current use from the Chang Chau Commissariat; [weight] seven mace, two candareens". Another specimen is of the same weight and fineness and besides the inscriptions on the obverse in Chinese and in Manchu, bears on the reverse "an effigy of the god of Longevity on the head and a tripod on the tail to authenticate its official origin."[1] These coins seem never to have gained any extensive circulation, and coinage by a government mint was not undertaken until near the close of the nineteenth century.

There was an attempt made to suppress these foreign coins together with the importation of opium shortly before the Opium War. The Provincial Treasurer sent a protest to Peking (1836) against such an action and declared that the coins were of great convenience to trade and unlike the opium were producing not the slightest injury to China.

[1] Williams, *Middle Kingdom*, vol. ii, p. 84.

The official showed that the coins had then an extensive circulation in the four coast provinces in the Southern part of China.[1] After the war all the different kinds of foreign coins were declared lawful money in Canton.

The carolus was but one among several kinds of dollars that were then in circulation. There were also the Peruvian, Bolivian, Chilian and Mexican dollars and the rupee. The South American dollars had been driven out of their home countries by the circulation of depreciated paper currencies, and a portion found their way to China. An official assay was made at Canton on the 13th of July, 1842, at a Spanish "factory" and the different dollars were found to possess the following relative values:[2]

To pay 100 taels of fine silver in Peruvian dollars it would be necessary to pay by weight....	111.455 tls.
in Mexican dollars	111.900 "
in Bolivian dollars	112.150 "
in Chilian	112.520 "
in rupees	109.790 "
in "chopped dollars"	113.207 "

Shanghai was made an open port by the Treaty of Nanking, 1842. It soon rose to be the centre of foreign trade of Central China. The carolus dollar was adopted as the money of account in this trade at Shanghai. There was a steady importation of the carolus dollars to settle the balance of payment. Mr. Morse states that in the year 1856 the import of treasure to settle trade balances amounted to $20,400,000; for the next year, $17,500,000 in silver. To meet this demand for silver the supply of the carolus was insufficient. This led to its abandonment as the money of account and the Shanghai tael was adopted instead in January, 1857.[3]

[1] *Chinese Repository*, vol. v, p. 419, 1836.

[2] *Ibid.*, vol. xiv, pp. 245-6, 1845.

[3] Morse, *op. cit.*, pp. 467-8.

The coin that has been the most popular in recent years is the Mexican dollar. Many competitors have appeared in the market but none have succeeded in displacing it in popular favor. The American trade dollar was declared lawful money promptly after its appearance; but most of these trade dollars went to the melting pot, being slightly heavier than the Mexican coin. The following are some of the principal foreign coins and their relative values:

The American trade dollar	27.215 grams[1]	900 fine	(24.4935 grams pure)
The Mexican dollar	27.072 "	902¾	(24.44 " ")
The French piaster	27. "	900 "	(24.30 " ")
The British trade dollar.	26.957 "	900 "	(24.2613 " ")
The Japanese yen	26.956 "	900 "	(24.2604 " ")

The carolus is now found only in certain localities on the lower Yangtze River. In these places it has obtained a scarcity value and is very much overrated, particularly in Anhui province where it commands a value sometimes 10 per cent higher than the Mexican. In most places all these dollars are regarded as so many parts of the silver tael.

IV. *Provincial Silver Coinage.* Silver coinage was first undertaken and a mint established for it in 1887 at Canton, not as part of a national currency system, but as a provincial undertaking for the convenience of trade. Before the close of the century several silver mints had been established in the provinces, all without the direct control of the Board of Revenue at Peking. The designs of the coins were different, and the quality and weight of silver used were not uniform. This was inevitable inasmuch as the Central Government did not exercise any supervision over the mint operations. The addition of these provincial dollars to the circulation further confused the currency conditions. Moreover, the silver mints, finding that there was a popular demand for the fractional silver coins, issued an enormous

[1] A gram = 15.432 grains.

amount of these minor pieces, greatly out of proportion to the output of the dollar pieces.[1] The mint at Foochow minted nothing but minor silver coins on account of the seigniorage profits. The result was that the fractional silver coins depreciated in terms of the dollar unit and have since been fluctuating in the local markets and circulating without reference to the standard coin.

The founder of the silver mint at Canton was Ching Chih-tung, then the Viceroy of the Provinces of Kuangtung and Kuanghsi. The circumstances that led to the establishment of this mint were as follows:

Since the close of the Taiping Rebellion the cash currency conditions had been very unsatisfactory, because of the general stoppage of cash coinage. The revival of industries in the provinces increased the demand for the cash currency. In Peking the 10-cash pieces had depreciated to about 2-cash in value and caused frequent price disturbances. Moreover the depreciation of silver after 1873 enhanced the silver value of the cash. Debased counterfeit coins appeared in large numbers and there was a gradual disappearance of the coins of better quality everywhere. These conditions led the Empress Dowager to issue an edict in 1887, commanding, in response to a memorial of the Board of Revenue, that "all provinces along the Yangtze and the seaboard be required to convert a portion of their remittances to Peking into cash and send this cash to Tientsin, there to be stored up in readiness for use in Peking; also that the provinces which were required by law to manufacture cash should one and all be called upon to commence operations without delay with a view to a gradual restoration to the old basis.[2] The edict seems to have been dis-

[1] The total issue of dollars was estimated at 40,000,000, while the number of fractional silver pieces was 1,400,000,000, according to a Government statement made in 1910.

[2] Emperor Kuang Hsu, *State Papers*, year 13, p. 1.

regarded by the officials. The complaint was that coining was too expensive, which probably was true. But the Empress was determined that something should be done to improve the currency conditions and these officials suffered degradation. By a subsequent edict the depreciated 10-cash currency in Peking was given a fixed legal value based upon the market value in 1887: namely, 2 cash for each 10-cash piece.

Chang Chih-tung, after this edict had been issued, determined to take steps to establish a silver-coinage system. In April, 1887, he requested the Chinese Minister at London to purchase for him some coining machinery. Accordingly a contract was entered into with Messrs. Ralph Heaton and Sons of Birmingham for the supply of a complete plant of coining machinery with all modern improvements for the production of silver and copper coins.[1] In July Chang Chih-tung memorialized the Empress suggesting the introduction of a national silver coinage, beginning the first experiment at Canton. Part of this memorial runs as follows:

The Povince of Kuangtung is the mart of Chinese trade with Europe, and the foreign dollar is the circulating medium not only there, but in Kuanghsi, Fuchien, Formosa, Shantung, Chihli, several of the interior Provinces, and the North Eastern frontier. Wherever there is an open port, the Mexican dollar is taken as the common currency. In this way the advantages to our Government of having a national currency of our own are lost, while they are being reaped by other countries. The principles governing the coinage of cash and of silver are the same—that is, they should both be made at our own mints and by our own methods, in order that we may maintain our national standing. In the Province of Kuangtung a system of our own coinage is especially necessary, as the currency there consists principally of old and mutilated dollars and broken pieces of silver, the use of which is a source of much loss to all concerned.[1]

Chang stated that he had already given orders for some coinage machinery for the minting of silver dollars and proposed the employment of a skilled foreign metallurgist to begin coining silver pieces in connection with the cash coinage. As to the weight of the coinage unit, he proposed a coin slightly heavier than the Mexican dollar in order to make its introduction easy. The coins thus issued should be receivable in the payment of public dues. He suggested that $1,000,000 in silver should be struck off at once as the first experiment and if these coins were received favorably $5,000,000 in all should be coined at Canton. If the experiment should prove a success he then would advise that the Board of Revenue establish a central mint at Tientsin to coin the national dollars. He estimated that if $10,000,000 per annum were struck the country would soon be supplied with the new currency which would be highly beneficial to China.

This memorial was referred to the Board of Revenue and nothing more was heard about it. The prospect of an early establishment of a national coinage was thus lost sight of. But Chang Chih-tung managed to secure sanction for his Canton mint. Thus the first provincial silver mint in China came into being.

This mint commenced operations in the summer of 1890. The whole establishment cost $1,000,000. The standard coin was fixed at 72 tael-cents in weight (Treasury tael) 900 fine. The fractional coins were of four denominations, namely, 50-cent, 20-cent, 10-cent, and 5-cent pieces. The 50-cent piece was 860 fine, the 20- and 10-cent pieces, 820

[1] *U. S. Mint Report*, 1887, p. 335.

fine, and the 5-cent piece, 800 fine. One-cent copper pieces were also minted. Counting in terms of the new silver dollars, about three million dollars worth of coins were issued during the first year; but only a fractional part of the total value was in dollar pieces. An analysis of the available statistics showing the outputs of the mint [1] (the first nine years) gives the following facts: Out of a total of 52,310,760.15 Canton silver dollars in value only about 3,000,000 dollars were in dollar pieces, the fractional pieces, mostly 20- and 10-cent coins, constituting nearly 95 per cent of the total output. This issue of a disproportionately large number of minor coins can be explained by an investigation of the demand for currency.

There seems to have been a natural demand for these minor coins. The cash is very insignificant in value. The silver tael unit and its decimal parts are not coined and the use of the bullion is attended with great inconvenience, while the dollar, judging from economic conditions, is altogether too large for ordinary use. No smaller coins that the dollar had previously been found in circulation. The British colony of Hong Kong had seized the opportunity to strike minor coins, and out of the colony's revenue of 1,557,300 dollars in 1888, 72,000 dollars was the profit on the small silver coinage on an issue of 910,000 dollars worth of silver.[2] These coins even commanded a premium in cash as high as 20 per cent. It stands to reason that the provincial authorities would seize the opportunity to increase the output of these fractional silver coins, considering the fact that there was considerable coinage profit. No limitations were put on the legal-tender quality of these subsidiary coins, such a conception being a totally foreign one.

[1] *U. S. Mint Report*, 1890, p. 275. All these sums are expressed in silver dollars of the new Canton standard.

[2] *U. S. Mint Report*, 1890, p. 275.

In 1895 the Wuchang silver mint was established by Chang Chih-tung who had been transferred to the Vice-royalty of the Provinces of Hupei and Hunan. An effort was made to determine a fixed ratio of exchange between the new silver dollar and the cash. In 1896 the viceroy issued a proclamation to the effect that the new Hupei dollar was officially given a cash value at the rate of one silver coin to 1000 cash. It was soon found out that a mere proclamation could not fix the exchange between the two currencies and the order became a dead letter.

The Peiyang mint was established in 1896. The question as to whether the tael or the dollar should be taken as the unit came up for consideration. It was considered that the tael would be impracticable. The Foochow mint was established in the same year. It coined nothing but 10- and 20-cent pieces during the 10 years of its existence. The amount annually issued was not regular: about 3,000,000 pieces in 1896; 2,500,000 in 1897; and in 1898 about 6,500,000 pieces.

It is not necessary to go into the details of the circumstances attending the establishment of the other mints. It is sufficient to point out the fact that with the exception of the Canton mint these mints were all established during the period of reform agitation after the war with Japan. By the end of the year 1898 there had been established no fewer than 10 provincial mints. Given in the order of their date of establishment they are as follows:

Canton Mint (operation began)	1890
Wuchang Mint	1895
Tientsin	1896
Foochow	1896
Nanking	1898
Hangchow (about completed)	1898
Nganking	1898
Mukden	1898
Kirin	1898
Chentu (projected)	1898

The provincial dollars never quite succeeded in displacing the Mexican and other foreign dollars. As we have already mentioned, the silver mints soon after their establishment devoted their energy to the coinage of fractional silver coins with the result that the latter depreciated. A dollar commands a price in these subsidiary coins ranging from 10 to 12 dimes.

The circulation of these coins both of foreign and of provincial mintage from the point of view of convenience of trade has been beneficial. But these coins have been in the nature of an "addition" to the earlier cash and uncoined silver currency. The double-standard metallic circulation described above remains essentially the same today as it was before the reform with some new "additions" which will be treated in the subsequent chapter.

Aside from the metallic circulation there is a considerable note currency issued by the banks and money changers current in local markets. Of this paper currency, a part is notes based on the cash. Such cash notes form a considerable portion of the ordinary currency. They circulate independently of government guarantee and almost any concern can issue them if it so desires. The notes are rarely current outside the district where the credit of the issuer is known to be beyond question. There is also an increasing amount of silver notes based on the tael or the dollar. Those notes issued by the foreign banks, particularly by the Hangkong and Shanghai Bank, circulate extensively in the advanced commercial centres.

To conclude: It can be seen from the above description of the currency conditions that even at present China has no uniform system. Economists attribute to money two distinct characteristic functions. They call it a medium of exchange, for it is by the use of money that exchanges are made in a civilized country. They also call it a measure or standard of value, by which they mean simply that it is the standard of prices. No one single unit of currency in the Chinese system, if so it may be called, performs the latter function for the country as a whole. The present conditions are the result of the *laisser-faire* policy. From the point of view of public welfare nothing seems to be so urgent as to reduce this tangle of systems with its shifting double-standard currency to a single system with one definite standard of value. A system of coins consisting of denominations adjusted to serve the convenience of trade, but all standing in a fixed relation to the unit of value, would secure the following advantages of which the present confusion deprives the public:

It would stimulate commerce and encourage internal trade development by enabling the business men to trade with the most distant parts of the country on a fixed basis of value.

It would greatly stimulate foreign commerce, which has been seriously hampered by the uncertainty and lack of uniformity in the currency used.

The greatest benefit, however, would result from removing the inconveniences and the confusion of the existing state of affairs. For monetary reform would substitute one system in place of many, thus making it no longer necessary to convert one kind of currency into another, each of which stands in no definite ratio to the other but fluctuates in the market just as the law of supply and demand dictates or the speculators wish to make it. It would relieve the business men and others of the necessity of weighing and testing and calculating, which the uncoined silver currency now makes unavoidable.

Considering China's exceedingly loose political structure, the enormous extent of the country, and the widely divergent local economic conditions, to introduce a modern system is no small task. In the following chapters we shall study the various attempts at reform which have been made since the Japanese War in 1895.

CHAPTER IV

Currency Reform

The modern reform movement began after the war with Japan in 1895. Led by a small group of energetic reformers who were readily listened to by the Emperor Kuang Hsu, the Government projected many comprehensive and radical reform measures for the modernization of the country. The movement for reform was rudely interrupted by the *coup d'Etat* of 1898 and a reaction came with the return of the rule of the Empress Dowager.

Among the reform proposals are found many suggestions advocating the introduction of a national currency system. All these currency suggestions are characterized by a lack of knowledge of monetary principles and of the actual conditions and needs of the country. The suggestions are in the nature of broad generalizations and are almost completely lacking in practical details. A few of them may be noticed in passing.

Hu Chu-fen, then mayor of Peking, was among the first to advocate currency reform. In a memorial [1] submitted in 1895 he suggested many urgent reforms, among which the reform of the currency was included. He urged the introduction of a uniform coinage system in three metals—gold, silver and copper—and the establishment of a bank of issue under the control of the Board of Revenue which was to have branch banks in the Provinces.

[1] Emperor Kuang Hsu's *State Papers*, year 21, p. 17.

Wang Peng-yun, a censor, made a proposal for immediate silver coinage to relieve the market stringency caused by the scarcity of the copper cash.[1] The question of establishing a central silver mint was taken under consideration. All the provincial silver mints, with the exception of the Canton mint, were established at this time.

Sheng Hsuan-huai, then a junior secretary in the Tsungli yamen, submitted a comprehensive reform program in 1896, which for the time aroused great interest. As to the question of national currency, he advocated the adoption of a coinage system based on the Chingping tael, 900 fine. He suggested that the central mint be established at Peking with four branch mints at Canton, Hupei, Shanghai and Tientsin. Taxes were to be made payable in the national coin and the use of bullion as currency was to be prohibited. Gold coins and fractional silver coins were also to be struck. He proposed the establishment of a bank for international commerce with a capital of 5,000,000 taels to be subscribed entirely by Chinese merchants. Of the total capital stock Sheng pledged the shareholders of the China Merchants' Steamship Co. to subscribe 1,000,000 taels. The bank was to be situated at Shanghai and to be known as the Imperial Chinese Bank of International Commerce. The imperial sanction was granted February 26, 1897, to Sheng and he was given authority, as soon as the bank had been established, to strike 100,000 coins based on the tael in accordance with his proposal. These coins were to be put into circulation as an experiment with the expectation that if the experiment should prove successful the coinage might be extended throughout the land. The powers and privileges conferred upon the bank were very comprehensive, including the right to coin money, issue notes, handle all govern-

[1] Emperor Kuang Hsu's *State Papers*, year 21, pp. 33-34.

ment funds and establish branch banks in the provincial capitals, the open ports and in Europe and America.[1]

Early in 1897 on account of the marked depreciation of the gold price of silver and the embarrassments of the Government in providing for the payment of interest and redemption of the gold loans, made to pay off the Japanese war indemnity, coinage on the gold basis found its advocate in Yang Yi-chih, a junior secretary in one of the Boards. Yang advocated the introduction of the English system of pounds and shillings with the gold pound as the standard coin. To keep gold within the country for currency purposes he suggested that the exportation of gold through the port of Shanghai be prohibited.[2]

With the exception of Sheng Hsuan-huai's banking project, none of the currency suggestions materialized into definite policies. The problem of currency reform was not especially looked into. Nor was this unnatural. It was but one of the many questions that were then claiming the attention of the Government, and it was relatively unimportant compared with the political and fiscal problems of the time.

The reform movement started again after the disasters of 1900. In July, 1901, the two Viceroys, Liu K'un-yi and Chang Chih-tung, in the third of their famous joint memorials[3] urging immediate reforms in the political and educational systems of the country and in the methods of government, took up the subject of currency reform and advocated the establishment of a national coinage based on the dollar unit. An edict was issued on the 26th of August, 1901, which was the first effective step in the attempt to improve the currency conditions of the country.

[1] Emperor Kuang Hsu's *State Papers*, year 22, pp. 31-33.

[2] *Ibid.*, year 23, p. 23.

[3] *Ibid.*, year 27, p. 51.

The edict ordered the closing of the provincial mints, except those at Canton and Wuchang, and legalized the circulation of the coins issued by the two latter on account of their uniform weight and fineness. Officials of the other Provinces desirous of obtaining silver dollars were directed to send pure silver ingots to either of these two mints for coinage. The closing of the local mints was intended to prevent variations in the coinage. The edict declared, furthermore, that 70 per cent of the tributes and taxes were thenceforth to be payable in silver sycee (fine silver), and 30 per cent in silver dollars, issued by these mints, at the rate of 72 tael-cents to the dollar. The Viceroys of Kuangtung and Hupei were commanded to issue strict regulations to the mint officers to give great care to the minting processes in order to preserve strict uniformity in the weight and fineness of the coins. Should irregularity occur the officers in charge were to be punished, and rewards were to be given to those whose work was successful. The mint officers were further required to render quarterly reports of the mint operations to the Board of Revenue.

The edict was well-intentioned. It was an attempt to correct the evil of varying weight and fineness in the issues of the different provincial mints, which was the chief complaint of the time against the silver coinage. But the remedy applied was hardly a satisfactory one. The enormous extent of the territory and the absence of modern means of transportation necessitated the establishment of several mints, and the proper way to secure uniformity was to establish uniform methods of operation and control over the mints by the Central Government rather than to close all but two. As a matter of fact, however, the edict was not taken seriously and the provincial mints continued their activities. Because of the absence of uniform regulations, and especially because of the careless and crude assaying, uniformity of weight and fineness in the silver coinage was out of the question.

To supply the insufficiency of cash in the Provinces, another edict, dated February 2, 1902, authorized the Provinces along the Yangtze River and seaboard to coin the new copper yuan, of which a small quantity had been recently struck at the provincial mint of Kiangsu. The new copper yuan coinage differs from the old cash in that it has not the square hole and is struck by modern coinage presses. The success of the new coinage was very rapid and an enormous amount was put into circulation within a few years. This issue yielded a considerable profit to the provincial government; but caused many hardships to the public on account of depreciation. The consequences of the new copper coinage will be discussed later. For the present, it is sufficient to note how the weakness of the political system, its decentralized and incoherent character, hampered efforts at monetary reform.

A series of international engagements gave added emphasis to the urgency of the reform of the currency. Article II of the treaty of commerce and navigation entered into with Great Britain, September 5, 1902, provides that "China agrees to take the necessary steps to provide for a uniform national coinage which shall be legal tender in payment of all duties, taxes, and other obligations throughout the Empire by British as well as Chinese subjects." [1] In the treaty of commerce between China and the United States, signed October 8. 1902, China made a similar pledge.[2] Currency reform was thus made a matter of international obligation.

A new factor meanwhile made its influence felt and for

[1] Emperor Kuang Hsu's *State Papers*, year 28, p. 25.

[2] *Ibid.*, year 29, p. 30, art. 13.

some time completely paralyzed the power of the Government. The steady fall in the gold price of silver became so serious in 1902-3 that it precipitated a financial crisis, and the Government on account of its foreign gold obligations was threatened with bankruptcy. In order to understand the situation aright, we must now direct our attention to its fiscal and international aspects.

The foreign indebtedness of the Government arose almost entirely out of two international engagements made in 1894 and 1900. The war indemnity to be paid to Japan according to the treaty of peace made in 1895 was 200,000,000 K'up'-ing or treasury taels. To this was added 30,000,000 taels as compensation for the retrocession of the Kuantung peninsula, making a total of 230,000,000 KP. taels. By a special agreement between the two Governments this sum was computed in English money and the payments were made in gold at London. By the 7th of May, 1898, the entire indemnity was paid off. the payments, including 1,-500,000 taels for expenses of the occupation of Wei-hai-wei, amounting to £38.082.884. With this supply of gold, Count Matsukata was enabled to introduce the gold standard into Japan in 1897-8.[1]

To meet the increased expenditure during the war, and to pay off the indemnity at its conclusion, there were two conceivable methods of getting additional funds, namely, increased taxation or borrowing. Increased taxation, for reasons which will be presently given, was not possible. The Government commanded no credit at home, hence foreign loans were resorted to. Four separate loans, amounting to £6,635.000, had already been contracted in 1894 and early in 1895, and the proceeds had all been spent in one way or another. Three much larger loans had to be raised in 1895-

[1] *Report on the Adoption of the Gold Standard in Japan* by Count Matsukata, p. 173.

1898 to pay off the indemnity. The terms were very easy, largely because of the jealousy of the rival groups of European powers with which the loans were made. These loans are as follows:

Franco-Russian Loan ....(1895)	4%	£15,820,000	(400,000,000 fcs.)
Anglo-German Loan .....(1895)	5%	16,000,000	
Anglo-German Loan .....(1898)	4½%	16,000,000	

To this gold debt was added what is generally known as the Boxer indemnity which was fixed according to the final Protocol of September 7, 1901, at 450,000,000 taels. This new indemnity was made a debt, payable in 39 years, bearing interest at 4 per cent. Reckoned at the rate of exchange of the time, the indemnity was put at £67,500,000 in gold.[1]

It remains to be seen what were the resources of the Government to meet the new obligations thus incurred. The annual charge including interest and redemption on the loans amounted to (about) £3,000,000. The annual indemnity charges raised the total to over £6,000,000, equivalent to (about) 40,000,000 KP. taels. The total revenue of the Government in 1901 was put at 88,200,000 taels approximately.[2]

A detailed treatment of the fiscal system and methods does not fall within the scope of this study. But a general outline will help toward understanding the monetary situation.

The principal sources of revenue are the land tax, the maritime customs, the leekin, the regular customs, and the salt gabelle. The land tax, consisting of a tax in money and a tax in grain, is a consolidation of the land tax and the poll tax and has been for centuries the principal support

[1] At the rate of 3*s*. to the tael, the total, including interest, will amount to 982,238,150 taels.

[2] Statesmen's *Yearbook*, 1903.

of the Government. Theoretically, the tax levied to-day is according to the rate fixed in 1713, exactly 200 years ago, when by an edict it was fixed for all time at the rate paid that year. As it is actually levied the rate is not at all uniformly adjusted to the quality and value of the land in different parts of the country. The lapses of time and absence of uniform regulations account for this. The confusion in the currency also works great injustice to the taxpayers and is one of the worst causes of official corruption. A word of explanation will make this point clear.

It has been pointed out before that none of the units of currency answer the description of a national monetary standard, that the cash and the tael are two independent units, and that the former is not a subsidiary division of the latter which is uncoined. The notes issued by the banks and money changers are of two kinds, silver notes and cash notes. The value of silver in cash or *vice versa* depends upon the supply and demand in the local market. The money taxes are partly collected in silver and partly, almost wholly in the case of the interior provinces, in cash. The transactions of the masses of the people are in cash. But the taxes are remitted to the Treasury in silver and the Treasury transactions are in silver. When the money is collected and remitted in different currencies trouble from the fluctuations in the rate of exchange is unavoidable. In actual practice the tax-collectors reckon on a surplus to make up any possible depreciation in the event of a falling exchange. This practice has the sanction of custom and official exactions in one form or another are usually made under this pretext. When the taxes are collected in silver, there is the chance of manipulating the adjustment of the local to the official rate of exchange and of exacting money for alleged difference of weight and fineness in the silver. The currency confusion affects all the taxes and it must be admitted that no fiscal reform can be carried out satisfactorily without taking this monetary aspect of the problem into consideration.

The maritime customs are the only revenue that is levied at a uniform rate and of which the amounts collected are accurately reported. The duty is 5 per cent *ad valorem* on both imports and exports. The tariff duties are arranged according to commercial treaties, and therefore the Government is not at liberty to raise them.

The "regular" customs levied on native shipping, *etc.*, yield only a trifling amount; but it is generally admitted that only a small fraction of the revenues collected is reported. Mr. E. T. Williams [1] gives a good example from Tientsin. The regular customs at Tientsin remitted to Peking, in 1900, were 70,000 taels; but after the station was taken under the supervision of the maritime customs this amount grew to no less than 1,195,015 taels in 1906.

The leekin, as the term denotes, was originally a duty of one per mille *ad valorem* collected in transit on articles of merchandise. It was a war measure first imposed by Lei Yi-ch'eng, the salt Tao-tai of the lower Huai River district, as a temporary expedient in the time of the Taiping Rebellion to supply the demands of the army. But it was retained and extended after the Civil War. There is no uniformity in this levy, except that it is many times one per mille. The levy oftentimes is a bargain between the collector and the payer. Corruption is prevalent and trade has been greatly hindered by this duty. Condemnatory edicts and memorials concerning it have been numerous in recent years and the Government has declared its intention of abolishing this imposition.

Salt was made a government monopoly as early as the

[1] *Quarterly Journal of Economics*, vol. xxvi, p. 912, no. 3; pp. 482-510, "Taxation in China."

seventh century B. C. by Kuan-tze in the dukedom of Ch'i (Shantung). The Government to-day exercises strict control of the manufacture, transport, and sale of salt, and for the administration of the salt gabelle the country is divided into ten districts, each with its army of officials and patrolmen. Illicit manufacture and smuggling are punishable by law. The officials are charged to see that the licensed manufacturers and merchants pay the proper fees and taxes and that they buy and sell at authorized prices and distribute salt within definite areas. It is said that the total product is not less than 25,000,000 piculs (133⅓ pounds per picul) per annum, and the revenue collected not less than 81,000,000 taels.[1]

These several taxes, together with the grain tribute and certain provincial duties and contributions, gave a total revenue in 1901 of 88,200,000 taels, divided as follows:

Land tax	26,500,000	K P. taels.
Maritime customs	23,800,000	"
Regular customs	2,700,000	"
Leekin customs	16,000,000	"
Salt gabelle	13,500,000	"
Grain commutation	3,100,000	"
Other levies	2,600,000	"

This revenue was quite inadequate to the needs of the Government; but the fundamental weakness lay in the decentralized system of administration. In actual practice the various taxes (except the maritime customs) had been provincialized and the Board of Revenue merely received quotas and contributions and held the provincial treasurers responsible for their regular remittance. The Government in short exercised only a supervisory power.[1] The fiscal practices resembled a feudal hierarchy. The Board of Revenue

[1] Under the Republic this revenue is undergoing rapid reorganization.

[1] The Customs Administration is an exception to this rule.

demanded a minimum from each Province. The provincial administration in turn demanded from the *fus* and *hsiens*, the administrative units, regular quotas. A large portion of the sums collected never reached the Government, but disappeared in one way or another at the different stages of remission. The published reports of the Board therefore could not give any clue as to the real amounts collected from the taxpayers. It rather represented a percentage. Aside from its abuses this established system had its fundamental weakness in its inelasticity. At an emergency the Government could only rely on the Provinces to forward additional quotas and requisitions. Such an emergency occurred in the war with Japan and again after the upheaval of 1900. The Board of Revenue made an apportionment of the new requirements in 1898 and again in 1901. The latter brought forth a vigorous protest signed by all the provincial governors and viceroys.

Such was the financial situation. The inadequacy of the old methods of taxation and the urgency of establishing an elastic system of revenue, independent of the provincial administrations, were made apparent.

We are now ready to examine the bearing of the fall of silver exchange, or the fall in the gold price of silver, on the government finances.

This fall in the gold value of silver after 1873 had occasioned many heated political controversies and hastened many fundamental alterations in the currency systems of several countries in the West. It was the subject of numerous international conventions and conferences. Yet until the opening of the new century it had little influence on the Government at Peking. It had always been a disturbing factor in China's foreign trade but, had it recognized this world-wide phenomenon at all, the then Imperial Government did not care to develop that trade which in those days was regarded as a concession to the foreigners. After the war with Japan the situation changed. During the six years 1895-1901, there had accumulated a debt of formidable magnitude, amounting in gold money to £120,000,000. The exchange during these few years had been steady. The rapid decline began in the latter months of 1901. In 1902 the rate started at 26⅛*d.* per oz., about 35*d.* to the Haiknan tael, and in November reached its minimum at 21 11/16*d.* per oz. or less than 30*d.* per tael. All the calculations of the Board of Revenue in apportioning the new expenditures were rendered useless. The uncertainty with regard to the exchange, or to use the more familiar expression, the silver price of gold, rendered the revenues deficient in the payment of foreign obligations and made the future doubtful.

A difference of opinion at once arose over the interpretation of the Protocol. Was it a fixed indemnity, namely, 450,000,000 HK. taels, or was it the equivalent of that sum in gold which at the rate of 3*s.* per tael (the rate prevailing early in 1901) was £67,500,000? This point was certainly not emphasized at the signing of the Protocol and might not have impressed the Chinese plenipotentiaries as anything important. It now meant a difference of many millions; for if it were a gold debt it would be at the new rate of exchange 2*s.* 6*d.*, the rate in December, not 450,000,000 taels but 540,000,000! The Wai-wu Bu (Foreign Office) opened negotiations and carried on a long-drawn controversy with the foreign ministers at Peking on the question of currency. Finally the dispute was settled in favor of the European powers.[1]

[1] Emperor Kuang Hsu's *State Papers*, year 30, p. 42. While the controversy was going on the difference accumulated into a new debt, which threatened to grow into huge proportions. The matter was settled in 1904. The interpretation placed upon the Protocol by the European Govern-

The financial problem of China closely resembled the problem that was facing British India in 1892-3. The standard of Indian currency was then silver, with the silver

ments was accepted. To render the effects of the fluctuations less annoying, it was agreed that the instalments should be paid monthly at the average monthly rate of exchange. The Government of the United States took China's side in these negotiations.

There could be no difference of opinion with regard to the loans made in 1895-8, which were explicitly gold loans.

GOLD PRICE OF SILVER IN THE LONDON MARKET (COMPILED FROM THE U. S. MINT REPORTS)

IN MONTHLY AVERAGES DURING THE THREE YEARS 1901-2-3

1901.	*Highest.* d.	*Lowest.* d.	*Average (Br. Standard).* d.	*Equivalent of a fine ounce with the exchange at par.*
January	29 9/16	27¾	28.9735	$0.63513
February	28 7/16	27⅞	28.1592	.61728
March	28¼	27 5/16	27.9495	.61268
April	27 15/16	26 15/16	27.2925	.59828
May	27⅝	27 3/16	27.4189	.60105
June	27⅝	27¼	27.4200	.60107
July	27¼	26 13/16	26.9629	.59107
August	27⅛	26¾	26.9375	.59050
September ...	27	26⅞	26.9650	.59110
October	26⅞	26⅜	26.6157	.58344
November ...	26½	25⅜	26.0913	.57150
December	25¾	24 15/16	25.4475	.55783
1902.				
January	26 1/16	25⅜	26.6250	.56173
February	25½	25 5/16	25.4140	.55711
March	25 7/16	24 13/16	25.0078	.54820
April	24⅞	23 5/16	24.3221	.53316
May	24⅛	23 5/16	23.6990	.51950
June	24 7/16	23 15/16	24.1850	.53016
July	24 7/16	24 3/16	24.3680	.53416
August	24 7/16	24 3/16	24.2259	.53106
September ...	24⅛	23 9/16	23.8750	.52326
October	23 11/16	24¼	23.4004	.51296
November ...	23¼	21 11/16	22.6925	.49731
December	22⅝	21 13/16	22.2067	.48679

rupee, a coin of the legal weight of 180 grains, 11/12 fine, as the monetary unit, established by a law of 1835. Until 1873 the average gold price of the rupee had been fairly steady at 2*s.* per rupee. During the subsequent 20 years the gold price had fallen till it dropped below 15*d.* The average for the year 1892-3 was 14.984*d.* per rupee while the average price for the previous year had been 16.733*d.* Meanwhile India had to continue remitting large sums to England, and as her revenues were collected in silver this sudden depreciation of her currency made the situation intolerable. The Government's calculated surplus of Rx 146,600 for the year 1892-3 was converted into a deficit of Rx 1,081,900 in spite of the increase of the revenue over the Budget Estimate by Rx 1,653,300. What Sir David Barbour, the Financial Member of the Indian Council, said in connection with this difficulty helps one to appreciate the corresponding difficulty of China.

The immediate effect of our financial difficulties and the cause which, by comparison and for the time being, dwarfs all others, is the fall in the gold value of silver, which has added to the Indian expenditure in two years more than four crores of rupees [a crore is 10,000,000]. If that fall could be stopped and the rate of exchange with England fixed permanently at

1903.

January	22⅜	21 11/16	21.9838	.48191
February	22 5/16	21⅞	22.1093	.48466
March	22 15/16	22⅛	22.5000	.49322
April	25 1/16	22⅝	23.3550	.51196
May	25¼	24 5/16	24.8894	.54560
June	24 9/16	24⅛	24.3300	.53334
July	25½	24¼	24.8611	.54498
August	26¾	25 5/16	25.6009	.56120
September ...	27 9/16	26¼	26.7524	.58644
October	28½	27 7/16	27.8935	.61145
November ...	27⅝	26¼	27.0050	.59198
December	26 7/16	25 3/16	25.7355	.56415

even its present low figure, the difficulty of dealing with the present deficit would be comparatively slight. The revenue continues to grow in a satisfactory manner; even under the influence of an indifferent season and poor harvest it has made fair progress. If we could feel assured that there would be no further fall in exchange, I have little doubt that increase of revenue, reduction of expenditure, with possibly some taxation of a temporary nature, would, in a very short time, re-establish equilibrium. A serious effort would no doubt be required in the first instance, but with a fixed rate of exchange we should have a definite task before us, and our measures could be regulated accordingly. But it unfortunately happens that unless some settlement of the currency question is obtained, there is no prospect of even the most moderate degree of stability of the rate of exchange. . . . .

Our financial position for the coming year is at the mercy of exchange, and of those who have it in their power to affect in any way the price of silver. If we budget for the present deficit of Rx 1,595,000 and the exchange rises one penny, we shall have a surplus; if it falls a penny we shall have a deficit of more than three crores; if we impose taxation to the extent of one and a half crores of rupees, a turn of the wheel may require us to impose further taxation of not less magnitude; another turn, and we may find that no tax at all was required. It will be obvious, from what I have just said, that what we have got to consider in making our arrangements for next year is not so much the question of increasing the public revenue or restricting that portion of the public expenditure which is under control, but the chances of a settlement of the currency question.

Later we shall have occasion to discuss the policy adopted by India. Meanwhile it is pertinent to note that with a sound fiscal system exchange disturbances are dreaded because nothing is more harmful than an uncertainty concerning the value of the tax yields. The financial difficulties of the Chinese Government, pressing as they were, would have been felt much more keenly had there been a centralized and responsible fiscal administration. As matters stood, the Imperial Government was able nominally to shift the increased burden upon the provincial authorities by increasing their quotas.

Of course, the effect of the disturbances of the rate of exchange between gold- and silver-using countries was not confined to India and China, but was worldwide. The first years of the new century saw fundamental currency reforms in many countries. The Government of the United States was the first to take action in the Philippine Islands, lately ceded to her by Spain. The currency conditions in these Islands were described as chaotic, and the Government of the United States after an investigation decided to reform the currency and introduce a new coinage on a par with gold. No definite action was taken until March 2, 1903, on account of the disagreement in the U. S. Senate.

Siam by a royal decree issued on November 25, 1902, adopted the gold-exchange standard by what is described as the "fixity-of-exchange" method.[1] The royal mint was closed to the free coinage of silver, and the government placed the tical on a gold basis by fixing its selling price from time to time. The rate was raised gradually; thus at the time when the mint was closed 21¾ ticals were equal to a pound sterling in the market, and the government made the first sales at the rate of 20 taels to the pound sterling. The selling price was soon raised to 19½ and in June of 1903 the government was selling at 18¾. The profits were set aside to form a gold reserve. The Siamese policy was largely based on the Indian Government policy.[1]

[1] Prof. Edwin R. A. Seligman, *Principles of Economics*, p. 508.

[2] Siam finally, by the gold-standard act, 1908, fixed the tical at 13 ticals to the pound sterling. A 10-tical gold coin, the *dos* weighing 6.2 grams .900 fine, was decreed the standard coin.

Great Britain and France took action simultaneously in their silver-using colonies, the former in the Straits Settlements and the Malay Federated States, and the latter in the French Indies. Each appointed a commission to devise feasible plans to reform the currency.

Meanwhile Mexico, next to China the largest remaining silver-standard country, proposed to the Government of the United States an international inquiry into the silver situation, and in taking this initiative the Mexican Government declared that its main object was to find methods whereby the stability of the rate of exchange between silver-standard and gold-standard countries could be established without thereby preventing the nations then using silver coin from continuing the same circulation. Some regularity in the purchase of silver, if possible, was also to be effected. The Chinese Government joined Mexico in inviting the co-operation of the United States.

The main point emphasized in asking the Government of the United States for an international inquiry and for assistance in inaugurating a sound system of currency was the injurious influence of the fluctuating rate of exchange upon international commerce. The immediate financial crisis in China was likewise a commercial crisis. China being practically a silver-standard country in her commercial relations, while the foreign countries with which she trades deal on the gold basis, the profits on each transaction depend largely on the exchange rates between the two metals every day at the London market. In the face of violent fluctuations such as those that occurred in 1902-3 international trade was attended with great risk. Mr. Alfred I. Hippisley of the Chinese Maritime Customs Service gives the following illustration: [1]

[1] *Report of Commission on International Exchange*, 1904, p. 183.

The value of the Haikuan tael was 3*s.* ¾*d.* in February (1904) and 2*s.* 7¾*d.* in April. Suppose a merchant invested £10,000 in tea costing 15 tls. per picul in February (one picul = 133⅓ lbs). His £10,000 would realize 65,850 taels, which would purchase 4,390 piculs of tea. Before this tea can reach Europe, merchant B taking advantage of the fall in exchange, also invests £10,000 in April in similar tea. His £10,000 realizes 75,590 taels, with which he purchases 5,039 piculs. The latter purchase having been telegraphed to Europe, the price of this tea will at once fall there, and merchant A will not be able to dispose of his tea except at a serious loss. Again, in February, exchange then ruling at 3*s.* ¾*d.*, a foreign merchant calculates that he can sell gray shirtings on the Shanghai market with a small profit, at 3 tls. per piece, and he enters into a contract to deliver 21,950 pieces at that price. He delivers the goods in April and receives his 65,850 taels. This sum represented £10,000 at the time he made the contract, but when paid to him it will only realize £8,711, so that instead of the profit he had calculated upon, he has to face a loss of £1,289, or almost 13 per cent.

The attitude of the Chinese Government on this subject was outlined in the memorandum which the Chargé d'Affaires Mr. Shen Tung handed to the Secretary of State of the United States, Mr. John Hay, January 22, 1903. The memorandum emphasized China's concern to promote wholesome trade relations with the gold-standard countries and pointed out that when the variations in the gold value of silver reached, as in 1902, nearly 10 cts. an oz. in gold in a single year, or nearly 20 per cent upon the price of silver bullion, this trade was rendered extremely hazardous and was threatened with destruction. Hence to establish stability in the exchange was urgent, and inasmuch as China had (1902) over one-third of the total trade between gold- and silver-standard countries the subject was one of large concern for the gold-standard countries as well as for

China herself. China's import trade was capable of great expansion because the trade then, though large in volume compared with the other silver-using countries,[1] was insignificant compared with her population, her enormous extent of territory, and her natural resources. If her foreign trade should grow as fast as that of Japan in the previous decade, an expansion of from $1.25 to $3.00 per capita, the imports into China would reach at the end of the decade $1,200,000,000. In inviting the co-operation of the United States to take the lead in an international concert of action, China's desire was to find the monetary causes which threatened the normal development of this trade. The memorandum goes on as follows:

The Government of China does not seek the restoration of the free coinage of silver by either the gold- or silver-using nations. It is recognized by this Government that bimetalism in the sense of free coinage of both metals is a policy which has been definitely discarded by the leading powers of Europe and by the United States, and that it would be futile to propose its restoration.

It is, therefore, not the expectation nor the wish of this Government that the gold-standard countries should take any action tending to impair their monetary systems. It is desired that the Governments of gold countries having dependencies where silver is used, and the Governments of silver countries shall coöperate in formulating some plan for establishing a definite relationship between their gold and silver moneys, and shall take proper measures to maintain such relationship. One such plan, it is reported, has already been proposed in both Houses of the Congress of the United States with reference to the Philippine Islands. It is this and other plans designed to accomplish the same end which the Government of

[1] The imports of 16 silver-standard countries (1902) amounted to $574,627,323. Those of China $196,934,342.

China would be glad to have considered by the United States and other Governments, with the view to the adoption of the best attainable monetary arrangement by those countries which are not prepared under existing conditions to adopt a currency system involving the general use of gold coins.[1]

The Government of the United States responded to the invitation of Mexico and China by an Act of Congress creating the Commission on International Exchange, March 3, 1903. The Commissioners appointed were Messrs. Hugh H. Hanna, Charles A. Conant, and Jeremiah W. Jenks. The Commission was directed to confer with the Governments of Mexico and China and also with the European Governments for the purpose of formulating some definite and feasible policy.

Meanwhile, in China an edict was issued on the 22d of April creating the Financial Commission and ordering the establishment of a central mint at Tientsin. The edict runs as follows:

It has been a recognized principle that the capability of a nation to exist as such entirely depends upon two things, the proper adjustment of its finances and the employment of competent persons. As the present situation is very critical, and the national finance [*sic.*] is in a great strait, the Government and the people are both suffering from this state of things. There would be no prospect of any improvement to be made in our fiscal policy unless this question were taken up and thoroughly studied in all its bearings, and such measures as are dictated by the necessity of the day were taken. We hereby command Prince Ch'ing and Ch'u Hung Chi, in conjunction with the Board of Finance, to consider carefully all necessary steps to make improvements in that direction and carry them out with diligence.

[1] *Report of Com. on Int. Exchange*, 1903, p. 45.

At present the silver coins used in different provinces are of different designs and quality, and their weight is also not uniform. This state of things entails a great inconvenience to the mercantile class, and it is therefore very imperative that a uniform device for silver coin should be designed, and a mint should be established in Peking [later Tientsin was chosen as a preferable location] for the purpose of such coinage. As soon as a sufficient amount of such coin shall have been turned out for circulation, all national revenues, customs duties, *etc.*, shall be collected and all public expenses shall be defrayed in that coin and that coin alone, with the view that the abuses of exacting money for making up alleged insufficiency in weight of silver ingots which are now used may be put an end to altogether. At any rate, uniformity must be preserved with regard to all the moneys received or sent out by the Board of Finance or by various provincial treasuries, and no new names [*sic.*] shall be invented for that purpose to create thereby divergencies.

We also command you to make exhaustive investigations as to how to frame satisfactory regulations, and submit them to us in regular order for enforcement. In short, this question is of great importance to our Empire, and will be of great benefit to the high and the low. You, a Prince and a Minister of the State, are required to carry this out with undaunted courage, unflinching energy, and strong determination, in order that our currency may be improved, and the benefit therefrom will be so widespread as to gratify our earnest desire to benefit our people by adopting necessary reforms. Respect this.

With the appointment of the Financial Commission in China the problem of currency reform was taken up in earnest. Yet the prospect of its prompt and satisfactory solution was not at all bright. The Financial Commission was not exactly a currency commission charged to investigate the currency conditions, and its members were not men particularly versed in this particular branch of knowledge.

The two officials, mentioned in the edict, were both high ministers holding important portfolios; Prince Ch'ing was the head of the Government under the Empress Dowager and Ch'u Hung Chi was then President of the Board of Foreign Affairs, the Wai-wu Pu. Moreover, nothing had actually been accomplished in the way of developing centralized governmental machinery to replace the loose political system. As we shall see presently the Provinces were continuing their independent coinage regardless of the will of the Central Government and the general interests of the people. The nature of the currency problem, both in its national and international aspects was but very imperfectly understood by the officials. The ordinary people did not even realize there was any problem at all. Without specially qualified men in the Government councils and without effective powers to put any comprehensive plan into operation immediate results could hardly be expected.

The currency regulations, which the Financial Commission was charged to frame, were not completed until two years after its appointment. The intervening events which will bring us a still closer understanding of the problem of reform in all its important phases may now be followed.

A special mission headed by Prince Tsai Chen and Natung was sent to Japan to attend the Osaka Exposition. Natung was charged with the special duty of looking into and reporting on the Japanese gold-standard system with the view to its introduction into China. The legations in Europe were instructed to participate in the conferences and discussions which were then being carried on by the American and Mexican Commissions with the European Government Commissions.

Of considerable importance at this time was the memorial of the Chinese Minister at St. Petersburg, Hu Wei-te, which may be considered before the American plan.

Mr. Hu's memorial[1] led to the first steps of the Financial Commission toward the accumulation of a gold reserve for the gold-standard system.

The American and Mexican Commissions had just completed their conferences in Europe at London, Paris, the Hague, Berlin, and St. Petersburg, and Professor Jenks, one of the three members of the American Commission, had been designated to proceed to China to present the American plan. Mr. Hu had previously been instructed to report on the discussions at St. Petersburg; hence the memorial, which was a strong plea for the gold standard.

Mr. Hu gave his reasons for favoring the gold standard in the following passage:

> The question of coinage is in itself a nation's own affair; but nowadays there is not anything in business, commerce, or government that does not mutually involve the people of different nations, which does not involve foreign exchange [*sic.*]. If the monetary systems of the countries do not agree, it is impossible to prevent loss. To have a good monetary system, a country must have a definitely fixed coinage, using gold, silver, and copper at a definite fixed ratio. The coins must be of the same pattern, value, and fineness throughout the country, if the best interest of the people is to be considered and it is desired to secure the faith of foreign nations. Those who have a gold standard do not, for that reason, suffer any loss in exchange, and international intercourse is easily arranged.
>
> Financial experts have estimated the year's yearly [*sic.*] output of gold, and there is no cause for concern lest it be not enough for the supply of the people of every country. As to the output of silver, there is no end to it. The greater the supply of silver, the cheaper it gets, so that the present high price of gold is not in reality that gold is dear [*sic.*] but rather that silver is cheap. China has made a practice of

[1] *Report of the Int. Exc. Com.*, 1904, pp. 190-200.

using silver, and consequently, using this as a standard, the Chinese consider that gold has daily gotten dearer. Other countries have made a practise of using gold, on the other hand, and hence, using this as a standard, they consider that silver has daily gotten cheaper. A gold-standard country is like a man who has accumulated riches to buy grain—if the grain is cheap, he reaps the benefit. A silver-standard country is like a farmer who has accumulated his grain and holds it for a rise in price—if the price goes down, he suffers. So silver-using countries and gold-using countries are in the same case as two people making a barter, in which one man's daily increase of loss (on account of his waiting each day for a higher price) is only the other man's daily increase of gain. Therefore, if we use uncoined silver for money we are in just such a case of barterers [*sic.*] with those countries which have a gold coinage, and it is needless to say which country is the loser. To use uncoined silver for money is like using uncooked rice for food or uncut cloth for clothing, for uncoined silver is nothing more than a product of the earth. Other nations consider silver merely as a commodity and not as money.

It is already hard to meet our demands, and hereafter it will be all the harder to put the country on a firm footing. At the present time gold is used in all nations throughout the world. Even among their dependent countries there is not one which does not use gold. Russia in Bokhara uses gold. England in India uses gold. The United States in the Philippines uses gold. England is now planning to use gold in Hongkong, and Russia has already begun to introduce roubles into Manchuria—just as if Manchuria were one of her own dependencies, as in the other cases mentioned. Why do they hasten so? Because when a country plans and marks out a frontier she must reckon upon its expenses—for is not the profit of her dependency the nation's own profit as well? It is equally evident that as the power of gold increases the power of silver decreases, consequently a country will spare no efforts or endeavors to regulate the expenditures so that her dependency will not be a burden to her. Where is there another nation as rich as China in land and subjects which would not speedily change her policy?

It is very evident, then, that nations which have not a gold standard, but keep on with silver at a debased value, will suffer. The system of coinage as adopted by the other nations has a fixed value in relation to each other, and although there are exchange charges, the market value is approximately the same, so that banks have no change to impose upon the people, nor have foreign merchants any opportunity for swindling. If China has a uniform national coinage, then she will be on the same footing with other nations, and there will be no cause for anxiety in the matter of exchange. The three metals, gold, silver, and copper, will have a fixed relative value; one silver piece being worth so many copper ones, and one gold piece being worth so many silver ones. Once fix the relative value, and it must follow that all financial affairs, large and small, will have some definiteness. Coins can then be used everywhere, far and near, at the same value. Officials and people can then use them without having them discounted for short weight. With everything uniform, business affairs will be easily managed. Rapacious underlings and dishonest traders will have no opportunity to squeeze.

Mr. Hu found that the opponents had eight objections to the gold standard, namely, (1) that the economic conditions did not admit the use of gold; (2) that China had no gold; (3) that the Chinese banks and cash-shops would oppose it; (4) that the officials and tax-collectors would oppose it; (5) that the provincial administrations would oppose it; (6) that complications would arise out of the indemnity payments; (7) that the gold standard might collapse on account of the unfavorable balance of trade; (8) that the Government did not have the necessary power and energy to introduce successfully such a reform. These objections were not all to the point; for instance, the third and the fourth arguments, which might be urged against any system of uniform coinage. The fifth argument was based on the fact that the Provinces were depending upon the coinage of silver and the copper coinage to make up deficiencies in the revenue. Whatever the standard might be, the practice of coinage for purposes of revenue must be discontinued and the Provinces must be prohibited from exercising the coinage prerogative.

Just as these objections were not strictly to the point, so Mr. Hu's rejoinders were mostly vague and superficial:—for instance, the answers to the first and second objections, which were at the time regarded as the main reasons why the gold standard was impracticable in China. He admitted that the economic conditions required the circulation of copper and silver; but he declared that the gold-standard system was not intended to replace copper and silver by gold as a medium of exchange and that the adoption of the gold standard was for the purpose of giving foreign nations confidence in China. But it is clear that if the silver and copper coins were to be based on gold an adjustment would be necessary. The complications of this adjustment to a new basis he completely overlooked. To the objection that China had no gold for coinage he merely answered that in inaugurating this system all that was needed was to let the other nations know that China had a gold reserve with which to maintain the fixed ratio between gold and silver in circulation and to prevent fluctuations. As to how to get the reserve he suggested that a loan must be resorted to. A gold coinage of 15 per cent of the total issue was needed. As to what the coinage ratio was to be he did not give any clue. Whether the gold could remain in the country he did not inquire, nor did he give any clear notion as to how the gold reserve was to be managed. However, this omission need cause no surprise when we understand what he meant by the gold standard.

The advantages of the gold standard having been pointed out and the alleged objections answered, Mr. Hu proceeded with the consideration of a plan of his own. His plan embodied suggestions relating to, (1) the name and weight of the coins; (2) the total amount to be coined; (3) suspension of the old coinage and the ultimate withdrawal of the old coins; (4) the manner of securing the necessary bullion; (5) the introduction of the coinage into circulation; (6) the manner of insuring confidence in the new system.

(1) *Name and weight of the coins.* The gold coin must be worth so many silver coins and the silver coin so many copper ones, each piece having its own particular name. The coinage unit should be called "yuan" in place of tael. He recommended that this new unit should have the weight of the Mexican dollars (72 tl-cents or 27.072 grams 902 7/9 fine). The tael he considered too heavy; and, besides, there was no such coin in use. The unit having been decided upon, "a table of values relative to gold" was then to be arranged; for example, 10 silver yuan were to be worth 1 large gold piece and 5 silver yuan one small gold piece. Fractional silver coins of one, two, and five-tenths of the yuan were to be coined. The copper coinage was to be made a part of the system.

(2) *The amount to be coined.* The population and the standard of living were taken as the criteria to determine the amount needed. An average of two silver dollars per capita, considered sufficient by currency experts, was recommended. The total would be approximately 800 million yuan. If one-fourth was to be coined at the beginning, namely, 200 million yuan, 15 per cent was to be made in gold coins, that is, 30 million yuan. In every 100 yuan there should be one gold coin of 10 yuan value and one of 5 yuan value; the remaining 85 yuan should be in silver coins. Uniform methods and designs should be used in the central and the branch mints.

(3) *The withdrawal of the old coins.* The old coinage must be stopped immediately and the old coins withdrawn. During the first years the Government should give full market value in taking back the old coins; but after 10 or more years they might be demonetized. The new silver yuan was to be 920 fine, the remaining 80 parts being the nation's seigniorage. On the coinage of 800 million yuan the profit would reach 64 million, with which the Government could not only pay its debts and cost of coinage, but also form a gold reserve.

(4) *The capital outlay.* A currency loan had to be raised to introduce the new system. Mr. Hu gave specific suggestions as to how the loan was to be negotiated.

(5) *The introduction of the new coinage.* When the Government had decided upon the date when the new coins were to be put into circulation the Government should make its disbursements in the new coins. Taxes also should be made payable in the new coins. As soon as the people became familiar with the new coins the system could be rapidly extended.

(6) *The manner of insuring confidence in the new system.* One way of securing confidence was to deposit the borrowed gold among the various foreign banks: thereby the foreign nations would know that China had gold in reserve. A periodical statement of mint operations must be prepared and made available to the foreign ministers at Peking, in conformity with the practice of other nations.

This Mr. Hu called a gold-standard plan; but it would be a mistake to conclude that it would have established a true gold-standard system. The crucial question is, Would the table of values of the silver coins in relation to gold be successfully maintained; that is, would the large gold coin always be worth 10 silver yuan and the small gold coin five yuan?

Now Mr. Hu made no mention of the coinage ratio, nor did he pay any attention to the measures whereby the silver coins could be maintained at par with gold.

Let us suppose he meant to accept the market ratio, and to maintain the currency on the gold basis. If such were his plan, the experience of other nations shows that the system would be deranged should the gold value of silver rise. The gold standard would be safe only if the gold value of silver should continue to fall. Such fluctuations as occur daily could not be controlled nor accurately foretold. For this reason it has come to be a binding principle for this particular species of gold standard to select a coinage ratio somewhat higher than the market ratio. The maintenance of this coinage ratio is the most difficult part of the whole system.[1] It is, however, reasonable to suppose that Mr. Hu did not see these complications and that his meaning was quite different from the above supposition. For in China at this date to coin silver and gold according to a fixed ratio, and to maintain the silver coin and the subsidiary coinage thereafter at the fixed gold value, was a strange notion. In the light of past practice and contemporary experience there is every reason to assume that the coinage ratio was no more than nominal and that there would be no efforts made to maintain the coinage par. What Mr. Hu actually meant would then amount to the issue of gold coins in addition to the silver and copper coins; very much as in contemporary practice silver coins were already issued in addition to the copper coins.

The value of the silver coins in gold, or *vice versa,* must in this case follow the market exchange ratio of the two metals, inasmuch as both were to be full legal-tender coins. The gold coins, should they remain in circulation at all,

[1] This point will be considered in connection with the American plan. See below.

would be just so many new additions to the silver and copper circulation. They might form a double standard with the silver, or more likely would resemble the gold mohur in British India, passing from hand to hand like a commodity, being bought and sold on the basis of the current market price of gold. It is evident that the consideration of the coinage ratio and the maintenance of that ratio is a factor of primary importance. By overlooking this point, Mr. Hu left the whole plan fundamentally defective and unworkable.

The Board of Revenue, however, was much impressed by the arguments advanced, and subsequently submitted a memorial which received immediate imperial sanction.[1] The Board proposed that a gold reserve be accumulated and that ultimately gold coins be issued *in addition* to silver. The Board emphasized the fact that it was to the great disadvantage of China to use silver when all the rest of the world has a gold standard. It further maintained that there is a large gold hoard among the people, but that this gold had hitherto been used solely in the arts because it had not been employed as currency. To obtain the gold supply for minting purposes was considered urgent; therefore, the Board proposed that the money paid in for ranks, titles and offices should be paid one-half in gold. Just how much gold was accumulated under this act is not known.

Conditions stood thus when the American Commissioner, Professor Jeremiah W. Jenks, arrived in China to submit the American plan.

The American Commissioner arrived in China early in 1904 (January) and stayed through the month of August. He presented the American plan to the Government at Peking; but before it was taken up and discussed in detail with

[1] *Report, cit.*, 1904, p. 201.

the Financial Commission he spent considerable time in visiting the principal commercial cities and the interior Provinces in order to study actual conditions. The special purposes of making this study were stated in the Report of the Commission as follows: [1]

First. To secure a general view of monetary conditions in China and of the methods of doing business under the various conditions found in different provinces. In the interior many days were passed in localities where no money is employed excepting copper cash and chunks of silver (sycee) which have to be weighed out by scales which each dealer or traveler keeps for the purpose. As opportunity offered, conversations were held not merely with officials of all ranks, but also with bankers, merchants, and even with day-laborers, local traveling peddlers, roadside workmen *etc.* In this way a reasonably accurate idea was secured of the methods of conducting business without any generally recognized currency and of the probable ability of the people of all classes to deal with a new and uniform money.

Second. Conferences with the officials from day to day, both those of high rank, such as viceroys and governors, and those of lesser rank, such as local district magistrates, gave an opportunity to estimate the qualifications of those in whose hands would need to be placed to a greater or less extent the administration of the new system when it should be adopted.

Third. The attitude of the people of various classes, officials, business men, and common people, toward a change in the system and toward the new monetary system suggested, was ascertained.

Fourth. Opportunity was offered to explain in part the main points of the system proposed to the viceroys and other leading men, officials, bankers, merchants, *etc.*, so that thus valuable criticism of the plans from the point of view of those familiar with local conditions was secured, and in many cases

[1] *Report of the Com. on Int. Exc.*, 1904, pp. 14-15.

opportunity was offered to remove from the minds of those who did not understand the purpose of the invitation of the Chinese Government or its attitude toward the United States in this matter the natural suspicion regarding the motive of the United States in undertaking this work; and, furthermore, objections which would naturally occur to those not familiar with the administration of currency systems, were overcome.

A pamphlet entitled *Memoranda on a New Monetary System for China*, containing the main points of the currency plan, was issued both in English and in Chinese and distributed. This pamphlet was circulated extensively among the officials, influential business men and the press. Later in the year, a second pamphlet was issued, entitled *Considerations on a Monetary System for China*. In it arguments in favor of the American plan and estimates of cost were presented in detail and objections to the plan were answered. It was pointed out that there were only two alternatives before the Government in introducing a national coinage system. The Government must begin either on the silver standard or on the gold basis. The American commission favored the gold standard. The proposals embodied in the American plan may be summarized as follows:

A unit consisting of a definite amount of gold was to be adopted. It need not be coined, but provision was to be made for the free coinage on demand of multiples of this unit. There was to be a standard silver coin, the representative of this unit. The bullion value of this silver coin, which was to be current with unlimited legal-tender quality, must be less than the par value to allow for upward and downward movements in the gold price of its bullion content. The coinage ratio recommended was 32 to 1, which was about 20 per cent higher than the market ratio of the time. The new coin must be received at its coin value.

To maintain the parity of this unit and its subsidiary coins with the gold standard the followng measures that had proved sufficient elsewhere were recommended: (1) Government control of the amount of the issues, so as to keep them within the demands of trade for legal-tender money; (2) prompt acceptance of the new coins everywhere in the country at their gold value by the Government in payment of public dues; (3) making private debts payable in the new coin; (4) the sale of drafts at or near par upon gold reserves kept at some convenient place abroad.

The first three measures were regarded as sufficient to maintain the parity of the coins within the country. The last measure was a provision for meeting the payment of obligations to creditors in foreign countries. Since in international trade what is needed to settle the balance of payment is a gold credit, it was considered sufficient to keep a gold reserve abroad against which the Government could sell drafts in case of necessity. A considerable gold reserve must be kept to maintain the parity of the silver coins. To obtain this reserve it was thought necessary for China to make a loan at the beginning. The high seigniorage profits from the coinage of the silver standard coins and the fractional pieces were to go to strengthen the reserve. As the chief means of replenishing this reserve after its reduction by the sale of drafts, the controller was to honor silver drafts drawn by the agents of the Treasury abroad in exchange for gold. Such transactions must necessarily take place, since it was provided that the money received in exchange for foreign drafts was not to be reissued but held in the vaults. The resulting contraction of the currency would make it more profitable to ship merchandise to meet foreign obligations than to withdraw from circulation legal-tender money which had acquired scarcity value. On the other hand, business men would find it more profitable to get the coins needed to meet their obligations in China by exchanging gold for the legal-tender silver coins at the Government bureau, or by purchasing silver drafts from the agents of the Treasury abroad. To secure the elasticity of the currency it was provided that the central bank should be prepared to issue a convertible note currency. Such are the main points of the system.

Evidently this system would require careful handling. The great difficulty was that China had not experienced government financiers competent to undertake the introduction of so subtle a plan. On this ground it was proposed that China appoint a foreigner as controller of the currency with sufficient powers and suitable associates.

It may be helpful to give the American Commission's own summary of its plan as presented for consideration by the Chinese Government.[1]

The Seventeen Suggestions

1. The Chinese Imperial Government promptly to take effective steps, satisfactory to a majority of the indemnity treaty powers, to establish a general monetary system consisting chiefly of silver coins with a fixed gold value.

2. In the establishment and management of this system China to invite and employ acceptable foreign assistance.

3. In pursuance of this plan, the Chinese Government to appoint a foreign controller of the currency, who shall have general charge of the system for China; he to have acceptable associates in charge of the mint or of such work as he may prescribe.

4. The controller to make monthly reports in detail of the condition of the currency, including amounts in circulation, loans, drafts on foreign credits, *etc.* His accounts (but not those of the general Government) to be open at reasonable times to inspection by accredited representatives of the powers

[1] *Report of the Com. on Int. Exc.*, 1904, pp. 80-1.

interested in the indemnity, provided the Chinese Government judges that such a provision would be wise in order to secure confidence in the system. Such representatives, as also the associate controllers, to have the right of suggestion and recommendation.

5. The Chinese Government to adopt a standard unit of value. The unit to consist of . . . grains of gold, and to be worth presumably, approximately, the gold value of a tael, or somewhat more than a Mexican dollar. Provision to be made for the free coinage of suitable pieces, multiples of this unit, 5, 10, and 20, on demand, for a reasonable coinage charge. Eventually some to be coined on Government account.

6. China to coin as rapidly as possible . . . silver coins, with an appropriate device, about the size of a Mexican dollar, for circulation in the country. These to be maintained at par with the standard gold unit at a ratio of about 32 to 1. More to be coined thereafter, according to needs, as indicated by provisions following. Subsidiary and minor coins, silver, nickel, and copper, of suitable weight and value to be provided.

7. Both the gold and silver coins to be receivable to par in payment of all obligations due to the Chinese Imperial Government in any of the provinces. When such obligations have been made in silver, the new coins may be tendered instead at their coin value.

8. The Government at its discretion, in conjunction with the viceroys, from time to time to declare, by proclamation, in the various provinces the new coins legal tender for debts incurred after a date fixed in the proclamation. Previous debts to be paid as contracted.

9. For the maintenance of the parity of the silver coins, the Chinese Government to open credit accounts in London and other leading commercial centres against which is may draw gold bills at a fixed rate, somewhat above the usual banking rates. For example, if the usual banking rate on London, under the system, were about one of the new coins for *2s.*, the Government might sell if the rate rose to 1.02 for *2s.* Such drafts to be made only under the direction of the controller

of the currency, but to be made on demand for all depositors of the new silver coins in sums of not less than, say, 10,000 taels.

10. Should it be necessary to make a loan for the establishment of a general monetary system with adequate exchange funds, it to be secured by sources of revenue sufficient to yield an amount which will provide for the needed interest and the sinking fund, such revenues to be managed in a way satisfactory to the parties interested.

11. The seigniorage profit from coinage to be kept as a separate fund. Whenever 500,000 taels worth shall have been accumulated, it to be placed as a gold deposit with the several foreign depositories in proportion to drafts made upon them. This process to be continued till at least . . . taels worth shall be in the gold fund on deposit.

12. For replenishing the gold fund after its reduction by drafts, the controller to honor silver drafts drawn by the foreign agents of the treasury in exchange for gold, at rates fixed by the controller.

13. Provision to be made for a banking law under which bank notes kept at par with the legal-tender currency may be issued by an imperial bank or by other responsible banks under the supervision of the controller.

14. As rapidly as is practicable the new currency to be introduced into the various provinces, the controller making use of the local governments, banks, business houses, and such other agencies as are best suited to the purpose.

15. Within five years the new system to be introduced into all the treaty ports, and as far as possible elsewhere, and all customs duties to be collected in terms of the new currency. Local taxes to be collected in the new currency as fast as it is adopted in the provinces, and provision also to be made for the keeping of the tax accounts under the new system.

16. The new system to be put into effect when . . . of the new coins are ready for circulation.

17. The controller and the representatives of the powers to be authorized to recommend economic reforms to the Imperial Government.

The American Commissioner argued that, if the national currency were first introduced on the silver standard and an attempt made later to put it on the gold basis, the result would be a great disturbance of business for a period of several years. There would be the necessity of raising the gold value of the silver coins in order to prevent the market fluctuations from affecting the fixed gold value of the silver coins. Should this be done rapidly, the banks and wealthy people would hoard great sums of money in order to secure higher rates. But if the rate were raised gradually, bringing it up month by month, there would be a period of unsettled business conditions. In either case there would almost surely be a commercial crisis.

On the other hand, if the monetary system should be introduced on the gold basis at the beginning, such a disturbance in the future could be avoided. Moreover, there were special advantages in giving the currency a fixed value in gold according to the proposed plan. These advantages were pointed out in the pamphlet called *Considerations on a New Monetary System for China,* as follows: [1]

I. *A fixed rate of exchange.* That this would be a great benefit was shown by the fact that in 1903 the Shanghai tael fluctuated in average monthly value from 2*s.* 1¾*d.* in March to 2*s.* 7*d.* in October, a variation of 5¼*d.* As long as these fluctuations affected the currency they would always seriously embarrass Government finance and international commerce. It was further shown that, by eliminating the element of risk and uncertainty from international commerce, competition of merchants would become normal and prices paid for foreign goods would be lessened. The result would surely be a great increase of China's foreign trade. The case of Japan was cited and statistics were produced to illustrate this last point.

[1] *Report, cit.*, 1904, pp. 119-123.

II. *Coinage profit.* At the prices of silver and copper then prevailing it was estimated that China could expect a profit of 20 per cent on the coinage. On the probable output of 250 million dollars within the first four or five years China's gain would amount to 50 million dollars. This profit could be made a part of the gold reserve.

III. *Increase of investments.* Because of the uncertainty with regard to the currency, business men had hitherto hesitated to invest money in China for fear of loss, except speculators and those who had political schemes to further. China could get capital to develop her resources from the gold-standard countries at very low rates of interest. This would be one of the decided advantages of adopting the gold standard.

IV. *Strengthened credit.* Not only would China be enabled to borrow more cheaply but it was also quite possible that some of China's foreign debts could be refunded at lower rates of interest. Should China be able to refund her debts which bear interest above 4 per cent at that rate, it would affect a saving of 3,136,400 taels a year (the tael taken at 2*s*. 6*d*.). This saving would be sufficient to pay the interest of the loan for gold-reserve purposes.

V. *Certainty regarding taxes.* The gold values of China's taxes had been greatly lessened on account of the decline of the gold value of silver. This fact made it increasingly difficult for China to pay off her debts. The danger of foreign aggression would be very great should China fail to meet her obligations. Under this proposed system there would be no further depreciation in the value of the taxes collected.

This currency system, a system consisting of a circulation within the country of a token silver currency of unlimited legal-tender quality and banknotes, both maintained at par with gold not by a gold currency but by a gold reserve kept abroad, is known as the gold-exchange standard system. It differs from a pure silver system in that the silver circulation is fixed and kept at par with gold. It likewise differs from bimetallism in that it does not aim at establishing a fixity of value of silver bullion in its relation to gold, but only to secure such fixity as regards the silver legal tender and the subsidiary coins.

The same system as was recommended to China by the American Commission was then being introduced by the United States into the Philippines, by Great Britain into the Straits Settlements, by France into Indo-China, and by Mexico within her own borders. Before we consider the circumstances which led to the rejection of the American plan, the history and development of this system may be traced with advantage.

The gold-exchange standard was first used in the Netherlands and the Dutch East Indies.[1] Free coinage of silver was suspended in the Netherlands in 1873 in consequence of the monetary changes in Germany and the countries of the Latin Union, 1872-3. For some time the Netherlands Government waited without action. A special commission appointed to investigate the situation made its report in 1872, declaring that "it would be impossible for Holland to retain the silver standard were all her neighbors to adopt gold as their standard of value." Meanwhile the suspension of coinage brought about the inevitable result that, while the gold value of silver bullion was continually falling, the silver coins appreciated as compared with gold. Finally in 1875 the gold standard was adopted at a ratio of 15.625 to 1 and the mint was opened to the free coinage

[1] Professor Jenks in his report as special commissioner of the War Department (1902) stated that the Scotch banks made use of this system in fixing the gold value of Scotch currency in the absence of a gold circulation for over half a century. See *Report, cit.*, 1903, p. 450.

of gold. In actual practice gold coins remained in the banks as reserves and the circulation consisted of silver florins and notes issued by the Netherlands Bank on the gold basis. Neither the silver florins nor the notes were legally redeemable in gold, though the Bank never failed to give gold for export purposes.

This system worked well till 1882. In the month of January, 1883, the balance of payment having turned against the Netherlands steadily, the Bank's stock of gold decreased from about 80,000,000fl. to less than 5,000,000fl. It is evident that had the stock of gold been exhausted the silver florins which were merely token coins would have became a depreciated currency. This experience led the Government to take precautionary measures and the statute of April 27, 1884, was passed empowering the Government in case of necessity to authorize the Bank to sell at the market price silver florins to the amount of 25,000,000, and with the proceeds to buy gold for replenishing the reserve. The statute has never been called into operation and the Bank's gold reserve has been steadily increased. Coinage of silver, except for recoinage and minting of subsidiary pieces, has been prohibited by law ever since 1873. For when the free coinage of silver was stopped the Netherlands had a stock of silver coins so large as to give the Government no small anxiety. Now the possibility of coinage of more silver florins is again being considered.[1] At the ratio of 15.625 to 1 such coinage evidently would yield very high profits.

[1] See *Report of the Bank of Netherlands*, 1913. The increase of gold coins and decrease of silver florins in the total specie stock in the Netherlands Bank and Java Bank are thus shown: 1900, *f*100,164,000 silver and subsidiary coin, *f*29,652,000 gold coin; 1913, *f*21,949,000 silver and subsidiary coin, *f*73,717,000 gold coin. The total metallic reserve on March 31, 1913 was *f*171,345,000 of which 94.29% was of gold and only 5.71% of silver.

The Dutch East Indies adopted the gold standard in 1877, largely through the efforts of Dr. Van Den Berg, lately President-Director of the Netherlands Bank. The Dutch gold coin, the 10-guilder piece, was adopted as the standard gold coin. The silver florins circulating in Java were declared legal tender in the Netherlands. The silver florins and the notes issued by the Bank of Java have been maintained at par with gold through exchange upon Amsterdam. In Sumatra and Borneo, however, the criculation of the many kinds of silver dollars, the Mexican, the Straits dollar *etc.*, continued, though of course no effort was made to keep these coins at par with gold. Hence the silver standard was actually in force in these places and even notes issued by private banks on the silver standard were enjoying a circulation unhindered. The gold-standard system with notes of the Java Bank on the gold standard existed side by side with the silver circulation. The Government transacted business on the gold basis but was willing to accept and even to make payments in silver at a rate slightly lower than the market rate of the day in order to demonstrate the superior stability of the gold standard. These two standards existed until 1907-8 when the use of foreign silver coins was abolished. These experiences have some peculiar bearing on the problem of reform in China to which we shall return in the closing chapter.[1]

In the successful maintenance of the gold standard in the Netherlands and particularly in the Dutch East Indies, sometimes in the face of fluctuations of more than 50 per cent in the gold value of silver, were laid the foundations of the gold-exchange standard system. The next country to adopt it was British India in 1893-99, though by a very different process. British India, June 26, 1893, closed the

[1] Dr. G. Vissering, *On Chinese Currency*, 1912, pp. 31-32.

mints to the free coinage of silver, the Government retaining the right to coin rupees on its own account. Rupees were made obtainable at the mints in exchange for gold coins or bullion at the rate of 16*d.* per rupee or 15 rupees to the pound. Public dues were made receivable in gold at the same rate. This action, intended to prevent the gold value of the rupee from a further decline, was taken on recommendation of the Indian Currency Commitee, commonly known as the Herschell Committee.[1] The financial difficulties of the Indian Government which largely were responsible for this currency reform have already been dwelt upon.[2] No definite action was taken to give India a fixed monetary standard until 1898. Embarrassed by the constant though slight fluctuations in the gold value of rupees, the Indian Government had repeatedly urged that steps be taken to secure the early establishment of a gold standard. The closing of the mints had not only prevented the rupee from a further depreciation, but had gradually raised its gold value until in 1898 it fluctuated about the fixed exchange ratio of 16*d.* per rupee. An Indian Currency Committee, known as Sir Henry Fowler's Committee, was appointed and reported unanimously for the adoption of the gold standard in India.[3] By an act of the Indian Government, September 15, 1899, the sovereign was accordingly declared a legal-tender coin in India while the rupee and the half-rupee remained unlimited legal tender, at the rate of 15 rupees to the pound. The committee also recommended that the mints be opened to the free coinage of gold, but this particular recommendation has not yet

[1] East India Accounts and Papers, *Report of Indian Currency Committee*, vol. xvi, 1893-4.

[2] See *supra*, pp. 65-6.

[3] Parliament Reports from Commissioners, *etc.*, *Report of the Indian Currency Committee*, vol. xxi, 1899.

been given effect. The gold reserve, the accumulation of which began in 1893, has been used to maintain the parity of the silver currency. Increased by profits upon the silver coinage as well as by the exchange of currency notes not only silver bullion but also for gold coin and bullion, these reserves have grown into an enormous sum.[1] The practice of giving rupees for gold has been continued. The reserves have always been available for foreign remittances, though the Indian Government does not bind itself to give gold for rupees. The policy of closing the mints to the free coinage of silver and of adopting the gold standard did not escape criticism, but the success of the Indian Government in giving the currency a stable value in gold cannot be questioned. The success, moreover, helped further to dispel whatever doubts there had been concerning the practicability of the gold-exchange standard system.

These experiences of the Netherlands and of India have shown that it is quite possible to introduce a gold standard without introducing an extensive gold circulation, and that a token silver currency with unlimited legal-tender quality can be maintained as the general medium of exchange and kept at par with gold through a gold reserve. Hence, at the time when reforms in the currency of the silver-standard countries were contemplated after the opening of the new century, the gold-exchange standard was widely adopted as a scientific currency system. The plan recommended to

[1] The Indian Government keeps two separate reserves, the Gold Standard Reserve which is kept in London and the paper-currency reserve kept in India. The total amounted on March 31, 1913 to £68,000,000 of which £27,000,000 was held in gold, £15,000,000 in rupees, and £26,000,000 in securities. Of this total £27 million was held in England and £41 million in India. This large sum is held (1) against a possible demand for cash in lieu of the paper currency notes and (2) to maintain the exchange value of the rupee. *The Asiatic Review*, vol. iii. no. 5, pp. 94-5, Jan., 1914.

China represents the latest stage in the evolutionary development of this system. As has been said, the United States Government introduced a similar plan into the Philippines, in 1903. The gold peso, consisting of twelve and nine-tenths grains of gold 900 fine, was adopted as the unit of value by the Philippine coinage act of March 2, 1903; and a silver peso 416 grains, 900 fine, at the ratio of 31 to 1, was struck as the representative of the gold unit in circulation with unlimited legal-tender quality. Silver certificates were issued against the standard coins held as security. A gold-reserve fund was created and kept in New York for the purpose of maintaining the parity of the silver coins with the gold standard.[1] The working of this system has already been described. The reform in the Philippines was completed, and the new system based on the gold standard was established within the short period of seventeen months.

In the light of historical evidence and contemporary experience, then, there is no doubt that the plan proposed to the Chinese Imperial Government by the United States Commissioner is theoretically sound and perfectly practicable. Nor is there any doubt that it is likewise superior to the alternative procedure of introducing the national currency on the silver basis and later raising its gold value in the manner by which British India adopted her gold standard.

The difficulty of the Chinese Government's position was that economic conditions within its country spoke strongly in favor of the silver standard, while international conditions, both fiscal and commercial, demanded the gold stand-

[1] The Indian banker A. M. Lindsay proposed to the Currency Committee of 1898 a plan called "a gold standard without a gold currency" which was not adopted in India. It bears close resemblance to the purest form of the exchange standard. *Rep.*. 1903. p. 449.

ard. The adoption of the gold standard seemed all the more urgent because by 1904 China was the only silver-standard country in the world. But a pure gold-standard system was clearly impracticable, since it was generally admitted that China had not the necessary supply of gold for the coinage of gold money. Looking at the problem in this light the proposed plan offered the best solution of the currency problem. The difficulties of introducing and maintaining this system must not however be overlooked and to these we may now turn our attention.

The most serious difficulty in establishing a system of currency of this nature in China arises from the use of token coins. Whether this difficulty would be really insurmountable and would defeat the system was a point on which expert opinion differed decidedly; and, as the plan was not then accepted and put into operation, it still remains a matter of oipnion and conjecture.[1] The circulation of token coins is a necessary feature of this species of gold standard. The reason is not difficult to find. To secure a fixed exchange value in gold for the silver currency the coinage ratio has to be higher than the market ratio, in order to eliminate the influence of exchange fluctuations on the gold value of silver coins and to permit a certain increase in the gold price of silver bullion without deranging the system. The American Commission proposed the ratio of 32 to 1 which was then nearly 20 per cent higher than the market ratio. This was considered by experts a sufficiently wide margin. Subsequent events have shown that even this ratio was too low and those countries that had adopted the same ratio, the Philippines, the Straits Settlements, Mexico, *etc.*, had either to re-arrange their system or change to a much higher ratio. The serious consequences of adopting a ratio either too high

[1] The British Commission, for instance, regarded the plan as unworkable on this ground. See *Report, cit.*, 1904, p. 33.

or too low were stated by the American Commission in the following language:[1]

There are certain risks in adopting a silver coin of a weight very much less than its bullion value, and there are risks of an opposite character in adopting a coin of a weight conforming too closely to the market value of the bullion which it contains. The dangers in the first case are much less serious than in the second. If too high a value is put upon the silver bullion in the coin,—that is, if the coin contains very much less silver than it purports to represent in face value,—then there will be a wide range of difference between the gold value of the coin as coin and as bullion. This is the case at present with the coins of the United States, issued at the ratio of 16 to 1; with those of the countries of the Latin Union, issued at the ratio of 15½ to 1, and with those of Russia and British India, issued at the ratio of about 24 to 1.

The two chief dangers in such a system are the private coinage of pieces of full weight and the strain upon national credit required to maintain the legal coins at their full value, since business confidence is an important factor. The first danger is not one which the advanced civilized countries have thus far found a serious menace to their monetary systems. The second danger has sometimes threatened them when, as in the case of the United States, the coinage was permitted to become too large. This danger would be much graver in the case of a country whose currency consisted chiefly of silver coins, without a gold circulation, and especially in one whose financial standing was not high. It seems to be desirable, therefore, in countries whose police system is not thoroughly organized to prevent and detect counterfeiting and whose credit is not of the highest order, to depart from the ratio of European countries and the United States and to choose a ratio more closely approximating the bullion value of the coins.

[1] *Report, cit.*, 1903, pp. 26-27.

It remains to deal with the opposite type of risk involved in the choice of a ratio giving too low a value to silver. This risk consists in the fact that under such a system a slight rise in the price of silver might derange the entire monetary circulation by making it more profitable to export the standard coins as bullion than to employ them as coins. If, for example, the Government of Great Britain, when the subject of giving stability to the currency of the Straits Settlements was first discussed last December, had seen fit to adopt a ratio corresponding to the price of silver at that time it would have adopted a ratio of about 40 to 1. This ratio would have given to the British dollar a value of about 40 cents in the gold currency of the United States. The rise in the price of silver which occurred in April last would have raised the market ratio between the metals to about 36 to 1 and would have raised the value of the silver bullion contained in the British dollar to about 45 cents. It is clear that the holder of one of these coins, if he had found its gold value in the Straits Settlements to be only 40 cents and its value as silver bullion at Hongkong or in London to be 45 cents, would have gathered up every such piece within his reach and sent it to the market where it could be sold as bullion at the higher price. The result, if such conditions had continued for any appreciable time, would have been to deprive the Straits Settlements of their currency and to bring great derangements into businss transactions.

In adopting the proposed system with its circulation of token coins the question would be, Would the Government be powerful and efficient enough to prevent counterfeiting from destroying the whole system? For, what was a source of profit to the Government would be equally an inducement to individuals for counterfeiting. Moreover, since the silver coins under this system would have a fixed value in gold they would necessarily have a fluctuating value with reference to the silver tael and the copper currency. These latter fluctuations would make the change from the old copper and silver basis to the new gold basis exceedingly difficult, even if the Government were powerful and the system intelligently managed. Of course, the danger of counterfeiting is unavoidable in other countries where token coins are in circulation; but it was claimed, and this must be admitted as quite true, that the danger was especially great in China because of the enormous extent of territory and the looseness of the political system. Moreover, the leased territories could easily be made use of as a basis for counterfeiting operations if the Government should successfully prevent them in Chinese territory. Another point that was urged against this system was that, unlike these other countries most of which were colonies, with a mother country always ready to come to the rescue in case the system should be threatened with collapse, China must rely upon herself for its successful maintenance.

However, these doubts were not primarily responsible for the rejection of this plan. What was regarded as the greatest obstacle was the necessity of employing foreigners to administer it. This was provided for in the American plan, and all fair-minded persons must admit that had China then adopted this particular system she would have had to depend upon foreign assistance, as she had not men with the necessary knowledge and experience to manage it. The system would not work automatically. It required skillful management, especially in the maintenance of the gold reserve.. The danger point of the gold-exchange standard system rests here.[1]

[1] The Netherlands Commission, speaking of the dangers that might be incurred in establishing a system of this kind in China, says: "Without magnifying them unduly, we ought to beware of belittling them, and our own experience has taught us that they are considerable. A system, if so it may be called, like the one now about 30

On the other hand, any attempt that looked like foreign interference in the finances of the country could not but be regarded with suspicion. This was not unnatural when it is remembered that the unsettled political conditions (the Russo-Japanese war was then in progress) and the weakened government finances created among the minds of the people a feeling of anxiety. What made the adoption of this plan immediately impossible was the opposition of Chang Chih-tung.

Chang Chih-tung's memorial,[1] opposing the adoption of the gold-standard plan, reached Peking shortly after the American Commissioner, Professor Jenks, had left it. The Viceroy Chang was then in a position of great influence. Aside from the fact that he was Viceroy of the two important Provinces of Hupei and Hunan, he had had a viceregal career of more than a quarter of a century, and was the recognized leader of the *literati*. Furthermore he had been a pioneer in the currency-reform movement and was responsible for the establishment of the first mint at Canton in 1887. His words, therefore, carried great weight and his memorial may be reasonably taken as voicing the official opinion of the time. In the following pages we shall attempt to analyze this memorial in some detail.

It is interesting to note at the outset in what light he regarded the mission of Professor Jenks. He was one of the few who knew of the invitation to the United States Government for the international inquiry into the silver question, but the invitation was understood by him as an

years in operation in our country and its colonies, does not work well automatically. That is the weak part of it. It requires constant supervision and in the first place intelligent co-operation between the bank (or the banks where there are many) and the Government. On this point too much stress cannot be laid." *Report, cit.*, 1903, p. 151.

[1] Emp. K. H., *State Papers*, Year 30, pp. 23-27.

attempt to *p'ing chin chia* or "to steady the price of gold." To him the American Commissioner was the United States delegate to China to *yi chin chia*, that is, "to confer on the price of silver."[1] The attempt "to steady the price of gold" was not so much a currency as a fiscal measure; for he stated in another part of the memorial that it had been intended as a "*plan to make provision for meeting the indemnity remittances.*"

These few remarks not only show his attitude towards the mission of the American representative but also reveal the very significant fact that what was then in the gold-standard countries regarded as depreciation of silver was in the silver country considered as appreciation of gold. To put it differently, the popular idea in a gold country is that the value of silver fluctuates; while in a silver country, the popular idea is that gold fluctuates.

The memorial covers the following principal points: (1) the inadvisability of employing a foreign controller; (2) the impracticability of the gold-standard system; (3) the benefits of adopting the silver standard for the new uniform coinage.

Objections to the employment of a foreigner as controller were made on the ground of national interest and were based on articles 2, 3, 4, 13 and 17 of the proposed plan. Thus he argued: "The finances of a nation constitute its life and no Government, be it weak or strong, provided that it is independent, ever permits its finances to be controlled by foreigners or allows foreign meddling." On this point nobody is inclined to differ from him. However, he most certainly misunderstood the purpose of those provisions and the cause of this misunderstanding lay in his

[1] In justice to Chang Chih-tung it should be said that his misunderstandings were partly due to the faulty Chinese version of Prof. Jenks's pamphlets.

imperfect knowledge of the whole plan of which the articles referred to formed a part.

His criticisms of the proposed plan are found in several passages. Thus, in describing the operation of the American scheme, he said:

What your minister cannot understand further is that in the proposed new silver coinage a gold price of 32 to 1 is arbitrarily fixed, alleging that profits amounting to about 20 per cent would thereby accrue to the Government in the form of seigniorage. . . .

If the gold price of 32 to 1 as fixed could be made to prevail both in and outside China, and if likewise China could reckon at that rate in remitting foreign indemnities [payable in silver] then it would surely be a proposition that is fair to all parties. But, according to what the said Commissioner has decided, the regulations concerning these silver coins minted at the ratio of 32 to 1 could apply only in places within the confines of the Chinese Empire; and in buying drafts or purchasing gold from abroad the value of the coins must depend upon the decision of the controller, who would accept the rate current on the day when the actual purchases were made. In the submitted Memoranda it was expressly stated that these silver coins are to pass at the ratio of 32 to 1 in China, but if payments abroad are made with these coins they must be valued according to their bullion contents, that is, at the ratio of about 40 to 1. This regulation would therefore compel the Chinese people to pay over to the Government a tael gold, worth 40 taels silver, as the equivalent of 32 taels silver, while foreigners upon entering Chinese territory could with 32 taels silver get the equivalent purchasing power of one tael gold. Even with Chinese silver to buy drafts or to pay for foreign gold, it would be necessary to give 40 taels silver in order to secure one tael gold.

Had Chang understood that in international relations the coins are and must always be taken at their bullion value and could he have recognized the distinction between the silver *coin* and the silver *bullion*, he probably would never have made such contentions and arrived at such conclusions. What was actually proposed was to give fixity of value to the silver coins as compared with gold, and not to fix the gold price of silver bullion, or the silver price of gold, which is something that no Government had ever succeeded in accomplishing.

From the above conclusions he proceeded to set forth the dangers and disturbances that would follow. He contended that the merchants and the people would not accept this system, and were this system put into operation arbitrarily, both the Government and the people would suffer great loss. Gold in the arts and gold products of the mines would be exported if the Government should decide to "buy gold at such a low price". Further on he argued:

> If the silver coins were given a token value, and if in the disbursements of the Government 32 taels in silver were made worth one tael gold (worth 40 taels of silver in the market), then the people and merchants would certainly advance the prices of their goods and their wage-claims from the rate of 32 taels to the rate of 40 (that is, an increase of 20 per cent).

But what he regarded as "still more tyrannical and unsound" was the provision in the proposed plan, requiring creditors to accept the new coins in the payment of old debts; and he predicted that, as soon as this order was put into force, there would be a total destruction of credit and stoppage of borrowing and lending followed by impoverishment of the people and great popular upheavals.

Enough of Chang's protest against the proposed system has been quoted to give an idea of his views and of the grounds of his objections. We may now look for the causes of his errors.

His conception of the coinage ratio. Theoretically, there is no reason to suppose that the proposed ratio of 32 to 1 was the only one China could adopt. China could choose any ratio she pleased, the American coinage ratio, the French ratio, the ratio of the yen or the rupee. The gold value of the coins bearing a token character does not depend upon the ratio or the intrinsic value of the coins, but primarily upon their redeemability in the standard. Practically, the selection of a suitable ratio for the silver in the coinage is a most difficult problem. In making this choice, both the ability of the Government to maintain the par value of the token coins and the possible fluctuations of the bullion in either direction, have to be considered. These principles have already been explained and need not be repeated. The proposed ratio, then, was one of weight between the new silver coin and the gold-standard unit. It must not be taken to mean that the value of silver bullion in relation to gold was expected to be fixed at that ratio—which would be a fantastic return to bimetallism, already given up by all modern nations as impracticable. To adopt a fixed ratio between silver coins and gold is quite a different matter and, as shown by the experience of many nations, is quite possible. The failure to understand the principle involved on the part of the Viceroy was due not only to unfamiliarity with facts, but also to his confusion of the *coin* with the *bullion*—a confusion shared by most of his people because of the habit of using silver bullion by weight as currency. That this was the case may be seen from his frequent allusions to the alleged unfairness of the Government's giving 32 taels silver for one tael gold, forgetting that what the Government gave would not be so much bullion but coins with a fixed value in the new standard of value—gold.

The grounds of his apprehensions. Much was made of the alleged injustice to the merchants and people. He did not seem to have a clear notion that the Government was not only to issue these coins but must also everywhere receive them at their coin value. The American Commissioner explained elaborately in his currency pamphlet that the Government could not by a mere edict make the silver coins really worth 20 per cent more than their intrinsic value, but that it could adopt measures such that people would not hesitate to accept silver coins at that value. We may quote his demonstration in full:[1]

A silver dollar which weighs seventy-two hundredths of a tael is worth in China at this date in American gold about 48 cents. If that same dollar or an equal weight of silver could be given by action of the Government a value of 55 cents American gold, it would be worth about eighty-two hundredths of a tael. The Government can not, by mere decree, make seventy-two hundredths of a tael worth eighty-two hundredths of a tael, but it can take other measures so that all merchants will readily accept it at that value. Exactly that kind of result is secured by all the civilized countries except China.

The following passages indicate the method of attaining this result:

If the Chinese Government takes seventy-two hundredths of a tael of silver bullion, coins it, and calls the coin the "imperial coinage dollar," it will be different in looks from any other dollar now in circulation. Let it pay this new coin to an official for 82 tael-cents; that is, if it owes him 8.20 taels, let the Government pay him 10 of the new dollars instead of $11.38 of the present dollars at the equivalent of 8.20 taels. The official will readily take the new dollars, at the rate of 82 tael-cents, under the following conditions:

1. The Government agrees always to take the new dollars anywhere in the Empire—Peking, Shanghai, in Szechuan, Honan, or elsewhere, instead of 82 tael-cents due in taxes or contributions or in any other debt due the Government. If

[1] *Report, cit.*, 1904, pp. 130-131.

the official can pay it to the Government for 82 tael-cents and the Government will surely receive it at that rate, he will not object to taking it.

2. The Government should pass a decree in due time, after the people understand the plans of the Government, saying that anyone who has a debt to pay to any other person may pay it in the new dollars at the rate of one dollar for 82 tael-cents. If the people know that the Government will always back them in paying their debts with the dollar at 82 tael-cents, they will not object to taking it at that rate.

3. If the Government says, further, that it will take these new dollars and give in exchange for them an order to pay in London or New York or Yokohoma 82 tael-cent's worth of gold for each new dollar paid into its bank, all the foreign banks will receive them at that value, for they are buying orders on those places every day. If the foreign banks take them at that rate, all native banks and merchants will take them at the same rate, for they can be sure of paying them out at that. If the Government takes them at 82 tael-cents, all the people will do so, for they will know that they may pay them out at the same rate.

4. The Government, too, having full control over the mints, will not coin more of these coins than the needs of business demand, so that the people will always be using all that are in circulation, and this will also keep up the value.

By following these methods the Government could without cost to itself gain a profit of 10 tael-cents on each new dollar coined. It would be practically as easy by the same methods to make a profit of 12 or 15 cents, and it would probably be best to make the gain about 20 per cent. It should be noted that this profit can be made on each piece only once, and that is when it is first coined and put into circulation. After that the dollar must be taken in by the Government at the same value at which it is paid out, so that there is no profit.

As 48 cents gold equals about 72 tael-cents and 55 cents gold equals about 82 tael-cents, it is shown above how a 48-cent dollar can be made to pass for 55 cents.

There is one point of great importance which must not be overlooked in this connection, namely, the consequences of demonetizing the silver long in use. Of course it was not recommended that this be done suddenly. Some years were allowed for introducing this system over the entire area of the country, and it was suggested that the Government begin in the principal commercial cities, or in one Province and then gradually extend it. As has been said, the crucial difficulty in adopting the new basis of calculations lies here: the coins issued in terms of gold would thenceforward have a fixed gold value, but a fluctuating value in terms of the old coins and bullion. For instance, the silver coin worth 82 tael-cents, mentioned in the passage quoted above, would not always be worth that much silver *bullion* but might be worth something quite different. Inasmuch as gold had not been used as currency by the Chinese, to popularize this system required intelligent management and was no easy task. These genuine complications arising from the adoption of a new standard of value, the Viceroy in his criticisms did not even recognize. All the difficulties he alleged were based on the supposed injustice to the merchants and people which would be imposed by the high coinage ratio of silver.

A strong plea was made in the last part of the memorial for the adoption of the single silver standard and arguments were advanced in support of it. He maintained that the countries in the West used gold currency because of their advanced commercial and industrial development, remunerative occupations and high prices. He maintained that the gold standard was not suitable for China on account of the wide difference in economic conditions. Chang described these conditions in different parts of the country as follows:

The people are poor, products of labor cheap, labor and personal service unremunerative, the common people economical in their way of living. Therefore the daily expenditures are usually reckoned in terms of the cash. A poor man limits his daily expenses to not over 20 cash, those of the well-to-do classes to not more than 60-70 cash. In the trade centres along the seacoast and the River Yangtze gold and silver, bullion or coins, circulate side by side with the cash; but goods from the interior, whether wholesale or retail, are always valued in terms of the cash. Although in wholesale transactions silver bullion is also used the cash is always taken as the standard coin. Generally speaking, in the cities of the Provinces of Kuangtung, Kuangsi, Yunnan, Kiangsi, Chekiang, and Kiangsu, 70-80 per cent of the business is done in silver currency, the remaining 10-20 per cent in the copper cash; in the trade centres along the banks of the upper Yangtze business is done partly in silver and partly in cash; in the interior towns on both sides of the Yangtze the proportions are 10 per cent in silver and 90 per cent in cash; and in the Provinces along the Huang River, 99 per cent is cash and only one or two per cent is silver. Considering the country as a whole, China is still partly silver- and partly copper-using; but the copper-using area exceeds 10 times the silver-using area. As a rule, transactions of the Government are reckoned in silver, those of the people yet mostly in the copper cash. For these reasons, although China is considered a silver-using country by foreigners, she is still in fact a copper-using country. She is therefore different from the foreign countries where it is suitable to use gold on account of a high level of prices and enormous wealth.

These conditions, he maintained, fully indicated that the silver standard was the most suitable for China. He said furthermore, that if gold became dear and silver cheap it would be a great encouragement to the development of the export trade, and consequently domestic industries would spring up which in the course of time would render China economically independent. Thus he added:

For the present we must begin the reform by establishing uniformity in the silver and copper currencies. The value of a tael in the cash should be made fixed and definite. The values of the silver and copper currencies must stand in a fixed relation to each other. If this is accomplished the benefit to the country and people will be immense. This is in fact what ought to be done according to the law of orderly progress. Then, when the currency has been made uniform, when silver and copper in the coinage have come to stand in a definite ratio, when the use of bullion as currency has been given up, when the order to prohibit the use of gold for ornamental purposes has been enforced, when products of gold mining have gradually increased, when within twenty years railroads have spread over the whole country, when silver coins have become universally acceptable, when consumption of native products has increased, when manufacture by means of modern machinery has pushed into the interior, and when the circulation of silver has reached even the remotest regions of the Empire—then investigate the situation and if it is indeed necessary to have a partial circulation of gold it may not be too late to consider attempting to introduce the gold standard.

The memorial as a whole was a powerful plea for the silver standard. Not only the plan proposed by the United States but any species of gold standard was regarded as impracticable in China. In Chang's opinion all efforts in this direction should be abandoned.

The above memorial was closely followed by another one, proposing the introduction of a uniform national silver coinage based on the weight of the tael, and suggesting that an experiment be made at Wuchang, the capital of the Province of which he was the Viceroy, with the expectation that, if successful, the system should be adopted for the whole country.

This latter memorial[1] embodied his opinions on the ques-

[1] Emp. K. H., *State Papers*, year 30, pp. 32-33.

tion of the coinage unit as the former on that of the standard. Official opinion was then divided on the question of the coinage unit; some favored the tael as the suitable weight, others preferred the weight of the dollar, which is 72/100 of the weight of the tael. Chang Chih-tung argued that should the dollar unit be adopted the adjustment, especially in the case of the land tax and the grain commutation, where the fractions are carried to the millionth part of the tael (*sze* and *hu*), would be exceedingly difficult. Arguments in support of both units were plenty; but the Viceroy decided that mere talk would not settle the question, so he proposed an experiment. His proposal was that the mint at Wuchang should coin tael-pieces according to the K'up'ing weight and that all definitive policies should be deferred until after the results of this practical experiment were known. To this proposal, the imperial sanction was granted.

Such vigorous representations made the adoption of the American plan impossible, notwithstanding the fact that not a few of the officials at Peking were favorably disposed toward this plan:—among others Chao Erh-hsun the President of the Board of Finance. The Government waited without action for the results of the Wuchang experiment. Meanwhile the currency conditions in the Provinces were going from bad to worse. Attention may now be turned to the activities of the provincial mints and their consequences.

The New Copper Coinage. The issue of multiples of the cash is a very ancient practice, the origin of which can be traced back to the earliest stage of China's monetary history.[1] The issues under the reign of Hsien-feng in the time

[1] It is recorded that a large coin was put in circulation by Ching Wang of the Chow dynasty (B. C. 544-519) because the cash was considered too light—Ma Tuan Lin, *op. cit.*

of the Tai Ping Rebellion, to which we have already referred,[1] were not an innovation, but merely a revival of an old practice. The new copper coinage must be looked upon as the direct progeny of these past practices, though unlike the old cash coin the copper yuan has not the square hole in the centre and is struck by modern coinage presses, not cast in moulds.

The proposal to coin the cash by modern methods was first made in 1897 by a censor by the name of Ch'en Ch'i-chang, who suggested that several denominations of the cash be struck by modern machinery and put into circulation.[2] The counterfeiting practices with the old cash had then become scandalous and it was suggested that coinage by the new methods would make counterfeiting much more difficult. Like most of the proposals of that time, it led to no practical action for several years. The new copper coinage dates only from the edict of February 2, 1902, which reads as follows:

> For some time past the legal currency in the various Provinces has been insufficient for use. Formerly the two Provinces of Fuchien and Kuangtung minted some large, round copper coins of excellent workmanship that were said, by the people after they were put into circulation, to be convenient.
>
> The Province of Kiangsu has now taken up with the same plan and finds it very convenient and beneficial, and moreover, a check upon the evil practices of illicit coining and illicit melting.
>
> Let the viceroys and governors of the Provinces along the River Yangtze and the seacoast provide the necessary funds and adopt the aforesaid plan and at once mint these coins in addition to the others being made by them, that they may be put into general circulation. The legal cash of the capital

[1] See *supra*, p. 32.

[2] The Emp. K. H., *State Papers*, year 23, p. 21.

ought also to be of the same sort; therefore, let the Provinces of Fuchien, Kuangtung, and Kiangsu at once forward to the Board of Revenue several hundred thousand each of the copper coins minted by them, that the said Board may pay them out and get them into use, which we hope will be beneficial and convenient to the people and prove a help to the currency. Respect this.

The copper yuan weighs 7.5 grams and contains 95 per cent copper and 5 per cent zinc. It was at first issued at the rate of 100 10-cash pieces to the dollar. Since, according to Kang Yu-wei,[1] the actual values of a tael silver and a dollar were then equivalent to 228 and 169 pieces in the copper coins respectively, the copper yuan was evidently a token coin.[2] The people took to the new coins readily and they were at first even accepted at more than their nominal value. The popularity of these coins and the profits from their mintage led to the rapid multiplication of the mints and increase of coinage machinery. Coinage of money became a *means of raising revenues.* The total issues for 1904 were estimated at about 1,693,700,000 pieces. The total for the next year rose to 7,500,000,000. At the close of the year, 1905, 16 copper mints had been established in 12 of the 18 Provinces with 846 coinage presses which, if worked to their full capacity, could turn out 16 billion coins a year.

This sudden and enormous addition to the circulation caused the coins to depreciate. The absence of transportation facilities made rapid distribution of the output difficult and irregular, while the congestion caused the utmost disorder and serious price disturbances in the local markets.

[1] Kang Yu-Wei, *Chin Pi Chiu Kuo*, vol. ii, p. 51.

[2] By some mints the copper yuan (10-cash piece) was inscribed as "worth one hundredth of a dollar" by others simply as 10-cash, or 10 mills.

Speculation in the coins was extensively practiced. The old cash, being undervalued in terms of the new copper coins, were rapidly disappearing from the principal city markets through the operation of Gresham's Law; the better ones were melted down and the inferior ones driven to the surrounding country. The copper yuan depreciated in terms of silver in Shanghai 22 per cent within the year 1905.[1] The conditions in different Provinces varied, but the depreciation was general.

Nominally intended to offer a more convenient currency than the old cash, the coinage thus resulted in a money-raising policy. This abuse was all the more glaring in view of the pronounced desire of the Government to reform the currency. The depreciation not only caused business disturbances but entailed serious hardships on the poor and the wage-earners who had to accept wage payments in these coins.

Bearing in mind these results of the operations of the provincial mints, we may now return to the currency policy of the Imperial Government.

The preliminary decision of the Government was reached and ten regulations for the reform of the currency, accompanied by a memorial in which the currency conditions in the country were briefly described, were submitted for the imperial sanction, which was granted on August 22, 1905. These regulations and the memorial were followed by another memorial submitting eight regulations for the central mint at Tientsin. These acts were results of two years deliberation on the part of the Ministers of the Financial Commission and the Board of Revenue.

The passages in the memorial relating to the condition of the provincial silver coinage were as follows:

[1] *U. S. Mint Report*, 1906, p. 191.

The first coinage of silver in China was undertaken in Kuangtung with the object of supplanting the foreign dollars and making good the deficiency in the volume of the copper cash. Afterwards the Provinces of Hupei, Kiangsu, Chihli, Chekiang, Anhui, Mukden, and Kirin successively bought minting machinery and proceeded to coin; but the coins minted differed considerably among themselves in weight and fineness, and even coins from the same mint lacked uniformity, so that the people made distinctions. The coins of one Province, too, were unable to circulate in another, and thus they were less satisfactory than the Mexican dollar, which circulated generally throughout the North and the South.

To remedy this situation the Ministers decided that provincial mintage of coins must be stopped. The coins were to be struck by the central mint but because of the enormous extent of the territory and the immense population one mint was considered insufficient. They therefore recommended that the mints at Tientsin, Nanking, Wuchang and Canton should be retained as branch mints for the coinage of silver. What seems to have given the Ministers the greatest concern was the copper coinage. Its condition was thus described:

Recently there has been added a minting of copper coins because of the shortage of the ordinary cash. The circulation of these has found favor among the people, and the profit from minting them has been very great. The various Provinces, therefore, have vied with one another in asking permission to establish mints, and there has been no end of confusion as a result. Because of this competition, too, recently the prices of machinery, copper, and lead have risen, and the worth of the copper coins has depreciated. If the provincial mints are to go on, each coining for its own use, each having its own way, perhaps the price will still further rise and the value of the cash still further depreciate, and after a few years the demand for the new coins will be fully supplied, their circulation will not be easy, and there will be a gradual loss on the capital invested. Moreover, in the new commercial treaties there is an article providing that a uniform currency shall be adopted, but if each Province shall be allowed to have its own coinage we shall probably be far from fulfilling the intention to have a uniform currency.

This being the case the proper remedy would have been to put a stop to this copper coinage altogether; but instead the Ministers declared that the Provinces were not yet supplied with a sufficient amount of these coins. Therefore they decided that for the present the local coinage should be allowed to continue, but that such coinage must conform to certain prescribed uniform regulations.

Nothing was said of the standard in this memorial and the regulations for the reform of the currency; but in the mint regulations were embodied the following general declarations: (1) The coinage in three metals will be known as "the Ta-ch'ing[1] gold coinage", "the Ta-ch'ing silver coinage", and "the Ta-ch'ing copper coinage". All three are designed for general circulation throughout the Empire. Again (2) "The original intention in the establishment of the central mint was the reform of the currency by issuing a currency in three metals, gold, silver and copper; but the establishment of a currency system is a matter of serious importance and we cannot avoid a careful investigation to determine the proper weight and fineness of the gold and silver coins, and this problem has yet to be thoroughly considered and decided." The question of the coinage unit was also left an open one.

Article 1 of the regulations prescribed rules for the control of the silver coinage to be put into effect *after the weight and fineness of the coins had been decided upon and*

[1] The name of the Manchu dynasty.

sanctioned. Four of the provincial mints, namely those at Tientsin, Nanking, Canton and Wuchang, were to be retained as branch mints of the central mint. Articles 2, 3, 4 and 5 dealt exclusively with the copper coinage. There were to be no more new copper mints; but those already in operation were permitted to continue their minting in accordance with a set of uniform rules. These rules specified that the copper coins were to be of the fineness of 95 per cent pure copper and 5 per cent zinc, and that the coins issued were to be in the following proportions: 10-cash pieces, 50 per cent of the whole number; 5-cash pieces, 20 per cent of the whole number, and 2-cash pieces, also 20 per cent of the whole number, 20-cash pieces, the remaining 10 per cent. The gross weights of the coins were to be: 20-cash piece, 4 mace K'up'ing; 10-cash piece, 2 mace; 5-cash piece, 1 mace; 2-cash piece, 4 candareens. The amount of the issues must conform to the actual demand of the market; interprovincial movements of the coins in large quantities were not to be permitted.

Article 6 required quarterly reports of the provincial authorities to the Financial Commission and the Board of Revenue. Article 7 dealt with the method of securing silver for coinage at the central mint. Article 8 declared that the coinage of money was a prerogative of the Sovereign and prohibited the merchants from asking permission to coin the copper yuan for profit. Article 9 declared that the coins issued by the central mint were to be of universal acceptability. Article 10 prohibited the prevalent practice of stamping and putting into circulation the Japanese copper discs, and required the mints to melt the copper themselves.

The one conspicuous feature of this Act was not what it decided but what it left undecided. On almost all the crucial questions the Government had not yet made up its mind.

Three months after the above memorials and regulations had been published, the Ministers of the Financial Commission and of the Board of Revenue submitted further and more definite regulations. In rejecting the proposal for introducing the new system on the gold standard the Ministers, in the memorial submitting the new regulations, declared that China's accumulations of gold were not large and that hitherto both in public and private transactions it had been customary to use silver and copper. Hence they deemed it unwise to accept the gold standard. In another place they stated that after the silver coinage had been successfully introduced into circulation, then they would consider the matter of accumulating bullion for the minting of gold coins.

Accepting the silver standard, the Ministers addressed themselves to the question of the coinage unit, which was then the most important issue between the contending parties, some supporting the tael unit, others the dollar unit. The choice of the Government was for the tael according to the Treasury scale, the K'up'ing tael. The Ministers, to support their decision, cited the opinions of both the Viceroy Chang Chih-tung and the Viceroy Yuan Shih-kai in favor of this unit. During the introductory stage not less than certain fixed percentages of all payments, public and private, were to be made in the new national coins. The subsidiary silver coins were to be legal tender to the amount of 10 taels, that is, to the value of 10 of the 1-tael coins. No limitations were provided on the legal-tender quality of the copper coinage. In other words the Act left the parallel-standard currency substantially as it had been before. The treatment of the copper coinage was left an open question until the provincial officials had made their reports concerning it. It need hardly be emphasized that for this reason the reform Act was not a thorough but a half-way measure. A special edict was issued sanctioning these new regulations on the 19th of November, 1905.[1] On December 7th of the same year the copper coinage was ordered suspended for a period of three months, awaiting results of investigations.

To recapitulate. Serious consideration of the reform of the currency began after the year 1900, largely on account of the changed political conditions and of the financial crisis precipitated by the fall in the gold value of silver during the years 1902-3. The Government of the United States offered its assistance and through the Commission on International Exchange suggested the gold-exchange standard system, the adoption of which was blocked chiefly by the opposition of the Viceroy Chang Chih-tung. In spite of all the efforts made during these years the Acts of August and November, 1905, were disappointing. In the first place, the copper currency question was left undecided. Again, no adequate provision was made for the treatment of the old coins. As a matter of fact these Acts, as we shall presently see, came to naught as soon as they were issued. The officials had shown very little appreciation of the magnitude of their task and little energy in coping with it, largely because of their inexperience and lack of previous training. The general attitude seems to have been that since the currency has been in bad condition for generations they could afford to delay yet for a few years. During this period there was no better example of the impotence of the Central Government than the abuse of the coinage by the Provinces in issuing copper yuan for purposes of revenue. Another five years had to elapse before a reform scheme was drawn up that was practicable, complete in its parts, and intended for actual execution.

[1] For the text of the act see Appendix II.

CHAPTER V

Currency Reform, From 1906 to the Revolution

The tael coinage Act of November, 1905, was never put into effect, the whole subject of the reform of the currency being subsequently reconsidered. Such questions as the standard, the size of the silver unit, and the treatment of the copper currency which had been left undecided, were all re-opened. Those who had favored the gold standard were naturally disappointed, but the real disagreement at the time was over the question of the coinage unit and of the fineness of the silver in the coinage of the standard piece. Many objected to the choice of the tael unit and held that the dollar (Mexican), 72/100 parts of the K'up'ing tael, being less heavy, was more suitable. Much time and energy was wasted over this question, apparently to no really useful purpose. For instance, the controversy centered on the question of the relative familiarity of the people with these two units; yet as a matter of fact neither the tael (K'up'ing, or Treasury) nor the dollar (Mexican) was universally recognized the country over as a monetary unit; hence in either case adjustments would be necessary. The proper criterion to determine the size of the standard coin was suitability to the economic conditions of the country; in this light the dollar or a smaller coin should have stronger claims than the tael, which is altogether too heavy. Indeed the tael weighs about as much as one and a half American silver dollars.

The disagreement over the question of the fineness of the silver in the coinage of the standard pieces was more serious. Those who were conversant with monetary principles pointed out that there should be free coinage of the standard coins either without charge, or subject to a brassage charge for covering the expense of assaying, loss of interest and the cost of the alloy. For these reasons the November Act fixing the fineness at 960, while the K'up'ing silver is 987-5 fine, was considered defective. The principle involved is a simple one. Should the people lack confidence in the system the coin would probably depreciate, while, if it was accepted at par value, the high seigniorage would be inducement to counterfeiting. The fundamental importance of this point the responsible Ministers failed to appreciate when the regulations were drafted. Disagreement over these questions together with the unsettled copper-currency problem offered ample opportunity and excuse for delay and inaction and the final reform Act was not drawn up and promulgated until May, 1910.

The Act of 1905 left the copper-currency question an open one, and operations at the copper mints were suspended for three months by the edict of December 7 of the same year. Under the nominal control of the Tu-chih Pu, or Board of Finance (a new name for the old Board of Revenue, Hu Pu) the minting was soon resumed. Issues from the mints continued to be steady and enormous. No attention was paid to the actual demand for cash, since, as has been explained, the coinage of these copper yuan pieces was depended upon as a means of raising revenues for the support of the provincial governments. Violent fluctuations in the silver value of these coins took place almost daily, and there were frequent complaints of the disappearance of the old cash.[1]

[1] Within the years 1906-09 the depreciation of the copper yuan currency was not less than 62 per cent according to a statement made in the British Parliament. *U. S. Mint Report*, 1910, p. 223.

The tael coinage at Wuchang undertaken by the Viceroy Chang

No accurate statistics of the issues of the copper mints are available and the exact amount issued, including the counterfeit coins, will perhaps never be known. Mr. K'ang Yu-wei puts the figures for the years 1906, 1907 and 1908 at 1,709,384,000; 2,851,200,000; and 1,428,000,000 pieces respectively.[1] There are no complete reports for 1909 when coinage was suspended in most of the mints. During this year the mint at Mukden emitted 10- and 20-cash pieces 23,609,267 in number, and the mint at Tientsin 138,387,500 in 20-, 10-, 5- and 2-cash pieces. The Government in 1910 estimated the new copper yuan coinage at a silver value of 100,000,000 taels. The disposal of the copper currency was provided for in the final reform Act of 1910.

The rise of the gold value of silver during the years 1905-07 put a premium on silver in meeting foreign gold obligations and relieved the Government for the time being of the anxiety which it had felt since the fall of exchange began in 1901. The steps taken to deal with this rise by those countries that had adopted the gold-exchange standard system are highly instructive and may be briefly reviewed.

The rise in the gold price of silver began in 1904. By November, 1906, silver had reached its highest point since 1893. In the Philippine Islands when the value of the silver peso reached and threatened to exceed its face value the insular Government passed an act, November 17, 1905, prohibiting the exportation of the Philippine currency.[2] This

Chih-tung as an experiment was not well received and the tael pieces, reported to amount to a total of 648,000 had to be subsequently retired and melted. The tael coin was described as equal to 37,300 grams, 3 millimeters in thickness, 41 millimeters in diameter and was of the following fineness: silver .877; copper .070; tin .053. *U. S. Mint Report*, 1906, p. 184.

[1] *Op. cit.*, vol. ii, pp. 51-2.

[2] *House Doc.*, 59 C., 1 S., vol. ii, Act no. 1411.

action was meant as a temporary expedient. The steady rise in the latter part of 1906 raised the gold price of the peso as bullion to 1.11, and notwithstanding the heavy penalties imposed for exporting, coins continued to be taken out of the country in one way or another, as the Secretary of Finance and Justice reported.[1] To prevent a serious contraction of the currency it was decided to decrease the silver content of the coins. So, in accordance with an act of Congress (June 23, 1906), the Philippine Commission (Act No. 1564, Dec. 6, 1906) provided a new silver coinage and fixed the weight and fineness of the new coins as follows: peso 20 grams of silver 800 fine, the subsidiary coins proportionate in weight but only 750 parts fine. For some time the two kinds of coins were in circulation side by side.

The Government of the Straits Settlements adopted a similar policy. It demonetized in 1907 the coins minted since 1903 and reduced the weight of the standard coin from 26.957 grams to 20.2172 grams.

Siam adopted a different procedure. She rejected the policy of decreasing the fineness and weight of the coin, but advanced the treasury rate of the tical by *2d.* from *1s. 4d.* to *1s. 6d.* The raising of the gold value of the tical caused considerable trouble in banking and commercial circles.

Mexico followed still a different course. Article XII of the Project of Monetary Reform provided that if the gold price of silver should rise so that the silver dollars should come to possess a metallic value equal to or greater than that ascribed to them by the legal ratio adopted, steps should be taken to demonetize the silver coins and to introduce the gold standard with the free coinage and use of gold as a medium of exchange.[2] The rise of silver in 1906-07 fur-

[1] *House Doc.*, 60 S., 1 S., vol. x.

[2] *Report of the Com. on Int. Exc.*, 1904, p. 422.

nished the occasion for this change contemplated in the law. Mexico immediately took advantage of the situation. The silver coins were exported to the amount of $85,956,202 and sold at a premium while gold was coined to the amount of $71,646,500 which went chiefly to the reserves of the banks. In this way Mexico passed to the "limping standard."[1]

The experience of these countries taught some useful lessons. In the first place, the necessity of having the margin between the bullion and legal value of the silver coin under the gold-exchange standard wide enough to allow for a considerable rise in the gold price of silver in the market was fully demonstrated. The difficulty of deciding what the ratio ought to be, was likewise shown, for what had been regarded as a safe margin in 1903, a margin of 15 to 20 per cent, was made to disappear by a steady rise of the bullion value. In delaying action the Chinese Government had thus saved itself from the additional trouble of modifying the system as these other countries were compelled to do.

Secondly, the experience of Mexico demonstrated the usefulness of the gold-exchange standard as a transitional currency system; for, if sufficient gold can be obtained to supply all the needs of the country, while maintaining the par value of the token coins, the country may automatically pass to the "limping-standard" stage of the gold-standard system.

As the settlement of the currency-reform question was delayed by continued postponement, many of the officials, particularly those who had to do with foreign relations, grew impatient. Early in 1907 the Chinese Minister at London, Mr. Wang Ta-hsieh (now Minister of Education in the Cabinet), memorialized the throne urging the adop-

[1] *Economic Journal*, June, 1909. Mr. C. A. Conant's article on "The Gold-Exchange Standard in the Light of Experience."

tion of the gold standard. The Board of Finance severely criticized this memorial and pointed out the superficial character of the arguments therein advanced.[1] In addition the Board of Finance announced an outline of the policy it expected to pursue. To this outline of policy we may now turn our attention.

The Board of Finance recognized the necessity of establishing the currency on the gold basis as early as possible. It declared that the pure gold system, such as is found in countries where the gold-standard coin is the only legal-tender coin among all the coins in circulation, the silver and copper coins being subsidiary and limited in legal-tender quality, was impracticable. Nor was the limping gold standard, such as is found in countries (the Uniter States, France, *etc.*) where some silver coins minted at a fixed ratio with gold enjoy unlimited legal-tender privileges, practicable in China. The Board found that China had not such a stock of gold as the adoption of the former system would require, and that the latter was not suitable because it is the result of historical circumstances not found in China. The gold-exchange standard was found to be the only feasible system. It must therefore be the aim of the reform. To attain this aim the Board found four possible courses to follow.

(1) To introduce the uniform national coinage based on silver; and subsequently to give the silver currency a fixed parity with gold; — the course by which British India adopted her gold standard.

(2) To introduce the silver coins at a fixed value in gold at the very beginning, and to maintain them thereafter at their gold value; this being the Philippine currency system.

(3) To introduce the system in a manner similar to (2);

[1] *Chinese Govt. Reforms under Kuang Hsu*, vol. x, pp. 51-56.

but at the same time to introduce a partial note circulation as a substitute for token silver coins.

(4) To introduce the new national silver coins on the silver basis to replace the old coins and bullion currency. Subsequently to extend the note circulation to replace the new standard coins; the coins so withdrawn to be held as a trust fund or sold for gold. When the note circulation becomes universal, to declare for free coinage of gold at the *market ratio* of a given time and convert the silver notes into gold notes. If the gold reserves prove insufficient at any time the notes may be redeemable in *silver bullion at its market value in gold.*

The last procedure the Board attributed to a suggestion said to have originated with Samuel Ingham, Secretary of the Treasury of the United States under President Jackson. Ingham had recommended that gold certificates should be issued in exchange for silver which was to be kept in stock. These certificates should be issued at the mints and the Treasury on demand. When they were presented for redemption the Government should give silver bullion at the gold value in the market. In this way it was expected to establish the single gold standard without serious difficulty.

The Board compared these four courses and found the fourth preferable because it combined the advantages of the others while free from the objections against them. In adopting this course the necessary steps to take would be (*a*) to prepare the necessary administrative machinery, (*b*) to put into circulation the silver coins, (*c*) to replace the coins by substituting a note circulation, (*d*) to recoin the standard pieces into subsidiary coins, and finally to declare for gold coinage at the market ratio of the day and maintain the circulation at that ratio thereafter. The essential thing as a preparation, the Board declared, would be to prepare a sufficient gold stock, to accomplish which would require six or seven years of strenuous effort.

This State paper is in striking contrast with the memorials and edicts that had been issued up to date. It indicates that the Board of Finance was no longer constituted of men without experience and knowledge as had generally been the case in the past. The course of action it announced as best, however, was not intended to be put into immediate effect. On political and financial grounds a bank-note circulation should be preferable to Government currency notes. Yet without a sound and strong banking system to extend and maintain it, such a course was indeed a mere theoretical possibility. For many years a metallic currency must be the only suitable one for the bulk of transactions in China, and the masses could not be expected to acquire the habit of using credit money in a short while. It, however, opened a new way of passing from a silver to a gold basis, differing from the procedure of British India.

Commenting on the policy thus outlined, the Ministers of State subsequently declared that the reform must be undertaken step by step, and dwelt at considerable length upon the difficulties of introducing this plan of reform. But nothing further was heard about their scheme, and the Government continued its policy of inaction.

Another memorial came from the special ambassador to the United States, T'ong Shao-yi, urging that the treaty provisions pledging the Government to reform the currency should be speedily carried into effect. This memorial led the Government to make another attempt to establish the tael coinage. An edict was issued on October 5, 1908, in response to a memorial inspired by Tong Shao-yi but submitted by the Prince of Ch'ing, other Ministers of State and by Prince Pu-lun and other members of the newlyconstituted Advisory Council.[1] In this memorial, the Ministers declared that the Government had, after consulting the high provincial officials, decided already for the silver standard; but that there had been some difference of opinion as to the size of the coinage unit. Eleven Provinces were found to be for the tael unit while eight were for the dollar. The Ministers reiterated their preference for the tael unit and sought to meet objections against its weight by accepting a suggestion made by the Viceroy Tuan Fang to the effect that half-tael, or 5-mace, pieces be coined in large amount to be circulated as unlimited legal tender together with the standard coins. The standard and half-tael pieces were to be accepted at their bullion value as pure silver, the expenses of minting to be borne by the Government and met by the profit from the subsidiary coinage. The latter was to be of two silver coins of one mace and of five candareens, 880 fine as against 980 fine for the tael and half-tael coins. These proposals were approved by the edict.

The whole proposal was a half-way and incomplete measure. Not a word was said either in the memorial or in the edict about the treatment of the old coins and the copper coinage. The Act suffered the same fate as its predecessor (Act of November 19, 1905), and was a dead-letter from the day it was promulgated. Meanwhile the Board of Finance had established a Bureau of Currency Reform for investigating the currency conditions and a widespread inquiry was conducted.[2] The final act was drafted and, after the imperial sanction had been given, issued in May, 1910.

[1] *Ch. Govt. Ref. under Kuang Hsu*, vol. x, pp. 60-62. Also *U. S. Mint Rep.*, 1909, p. 248.

[2] Mr. Tong Shao-yi upon his return from the United States made a series of suggestions on the questions of currency reform to the Board of Finance. These suggestions were on five heads, namely,

The currency-reform measures of May, 1910,[1] consisted of an edict issued on the 16th of the 4th month, the second year of Hsuan Tung (May 24, 1910), and a series of regulations and memorials. The edict stated that the Government had decided that for the present silver was to be the standard and the unit of the currency was to be the *yuan*, in gross weight 72/100 of the K'up'ing tael (reckoned at 37.301 grams), that is, 26.856 grams, 900 fine, the weight in fine silver being 648/1000 K'up'ing tael. Thus the previous decision to base the currency on the K'up'ing tael unit was reversed. Subsidiary coins in silver, nickel and copper, on the decimal system, were provided. The new coins must be used in the payment of dues, public or private, and the old coins and bullion were to be permitted to circulate only within a prescribed limit of time. The old coins were to be exchanged for the new ones by the Government Bank and the mints, and timely preparations were to be made for this exchange. Refusal to accept the national coinage or to force its acceptance at a discount was to be an unlawful act.

the standard, the size of the silver coin, the fineness of the silver in the coinage, the subsidiary coinage, and the treatment of the existing copper currency. On the question of the standard Mr. Tong reached the conclusion that the reform had best begin on the silver-standard basis, but with the ultimate aim of attaining the gold standard. He found that the gold-exchange standard would be very difficult to enforce in China, and that the difficulty was that the token coins under this system would be continually fluctuating in terms of the silver bullion. Again, he feared that the coins might depreciate through over-issue for the seigniorage. He favored the adoption of a unit of the weight of the dollar. On the question of the treatment of the copper currency Mr. Tong suggested that the new coins should be used to retire the old, and pointed out the fault of the previous Acts in not including the copper currency in the reform considerations but treating it as an independent system by itself.

[1] For the text of the Act see Appendix III.

Provisions were made for the first time for the treatment of the old coins. These provisions were embodied in a separate memorial of the Board of Finance. In this memorial the Board submitted its findings about the silver and copper coinages. The silver dollars coined at the provincial mints were estimated at 40,000,000 and the number of fractional silver coins, mostly 10- and 20-cent pieces, at the enormous sum of 1,400,000,000. To retire them by exchanging them for the new coins would, as the Board estimated, entail a loss of 20,000,000 yuan in the five items of inferior touch, exchange, transportation, refining and loss of interest. This cost the Government was not prepared to face. As an alternative plan the Board decided that, when the new coins were being introduced, the old silver coins both large and small should continue to circulate for a time at their market value. At the same time they were to be gradually redeemed at the market rate and reminted into the new coins. After the new coins had been issued in sufficient quantities, a definite date was to be fixed for stopping the circulation of the old coins and they must thereafter be exchanged for the new coins according to their bullion value.

The treatment of the copper coinage the Board considered as the most difficult problem. The total value of these copper yuans in silver was estimated at 100,000,000 taels. The Board declared that in dealing with these coins both the interest of the Government and that of the people must be considered. One of the plans suggested was to withdraw and remint them into the new coinage; another was to restore the original decimal value of these copper coins. Both of these plans the Board regarded as impracticable; the former because of the expense involved and because of the necessity of depressing the value of the coins in order to get a return to cover the reminting expenses; the latter because of the necessity of raising the value of the coins so that the market value might be made equal to the legal value. The policy decided upon was that the copper coins were to be permitted to circulate for a limited period of time while the new coins were being introduced. Proclamations were to be issued by the authorities to the effect that the old coins were to be legal tender to the amount of three yuan from the date the new coins were issued, and in the second year to the amount of one yuan. At the same time the Board was to take measures to redeem the coins and remint them to the requisite amount as 2-cent and 5-mill subsidiary coins. The best 10-cash pieces might also be selected to serve as 1-cent subsidiary coins in the new system. Subsequently, at a suitable time, the Board should announce that the old copper coins were to be regarded as subsidiary coins or to be forbidden to circulate altogether.

The proposed method of treating the old coins was severely criticized by Liang C'hi-ch'ao [1] on the ground that it was silent about the foreign coins then in the hands of the Chinese people (estimated at over 100,000,000 dollars). He further contended that the amount of provincial dollars was over-estimated, and that the Government ought to redeem these coins at their face value. Again, he made the point that the dollars and the minor silver coins ought to have been separately treated. The only feasible and justifiable policy in the withdrawal of these silver and copper subsidiary coins, which were all circulating at different rates of discount at different places, would be for the Government to exchange them for the new coins within a prescribed period of time at their actual market values. Otherwise serious speculations and business disturbances would be unpreventable.

[1] *Kuo Feng Pao*, see *infra*, p. 141.

Special regulations were also drawn up by the Board of Finance for the reorganization of the Bank of Issue and for the issue of convertible banknotes. Article 3 of the Bank Regulations provided that the Bank should keep on hand for the redemption of the notes cash reserves of 50 per cent of the total issue; the other 50 per cent to be covered by marketable securities. In addition to the funds for the note redemption the Bank was to keep on hand a cash reserve of 25 per cent of deposits on current account and time deposits of under two months. It was further provided (Article 6) that at times of financial stringency in the market the Bank should issue notes in excess of the limit provided for in Article 3, but the approval of the Board of Finance must be first obtained, and on all the paper issued in excess of the limit a tax of 6 per cent per annum must be paid, or such rate as might be determined by the Board of Finance at the time. In case of oversupply of the note currency, the Bank was to be ordered by the Board to take measures to reduce the circulation. The note-issue privilege was to be the Bank's monopoly.

Concluding remarks. It looked as if the reform was at last to be launched. Those who had followed the course of events and appreciated the difficulties of introducing the gold standard seemed to be satisfied with the decision of the Government to introduce the national coinage system on the silver basis as the preliminary step of the reform. There must always be something to debate about as long as the Government hesitated to act; for each system had its merits. It is evident that even if the system was introduced on the silver standard the benefits that would be derived from reducing the existing chaos to order would be immense. For the reform of the currency an agreement was signed on April 15, 1911, between Duke Tsai Tze as President of the Board of Finance as the first party, and Messrs. Willard

Straight (representing Messrs. J. P. Morgan & Co., Kuhn, Loeb & Co., the First National Bank, and the National City Bank, all of New York, constituting the American Group), E. G. Hillier (for the Hongkong and Shanghai Banking Corporation), H. Cordes (for the Deutsche-Asiatische Bank), and MM. Cazenave and Henry Mazot (representing the Banque de l'Indo Chine) as the second party, authorizing the issue by the International Group of a 5-per cent Sinking Fund Gold Loan of £10,000,000, the issue price to be 95.

According to the terms of the agreement, the Chinese Government was to engage a foreign expert to assist the Bureau of Currency Reform. Dr. G. Vissering, then President of the Bank of Java, now President of the Netherlands Bank, was accordingly appointed by the Chinese Government as Monetary Adviser. The loan was not floated on account of the Revolution in China. This Revolution which broke out at Wuchang on October 10, 1911, resulted in the downfall of the Manchu dynasty and the establishment of the Republican form of government. The National Coinage Act had not become fully operative when the Revolution began and under the Republic the reform policy has been reconsidered. A considerable amount of silver coins, the *yuan* and its subsidiary pieces, has been put into circulation, though the definite amount is not known.

APPENDIX I

SINCE the Revolution, currency conditions have become a great deal worse than before on account of the issues by the provincial and local authorities of a large amount of paper currency. The exact amount is not accurately known, but is estimated at approximately 130,000,000 silver dollars. The paper has been heavily discounted. The degree of depreciation varies in different places. The paper currency is based on the double standard, that is, there are silver as well as cash notes.

The depreciation is heaviest in Kuangtung where the total issue was estimated at between $22,000,000 silver (the Government estimate) and $12,000,000 (the estimate according to the provincial authorities). In December, 1913, the paper was being received at 43 per cent of its face value. Kiangsi is another Province where the paper has suffered heavy discount. Silver has practically given way to paper and the copper yuan, and disappeared. A large amount of the copper yuan has been put into circulation during the last two years in this Province. It was reported that in 1912 the cash pieces fluctuated from .538 Changsha taels per 100 at the beginning of January to .70 Changsha taels per 100 at the end of December and that the rise in the value of the cash indicated the depreciation of the paper money which had meanwhile displaced silver.[1] The issue in this Province was estimated at between $21,000,000 and $14,694,000. Sze-chuan is in a similar situation. Last December the

[1] The *China Rep.*, weekly ed., Aug. 22, 1913.

paper dollar was exchanged at Chentu for 950 to 1000 cash, while the silver dollar was at 1300 to 1350.[1] The depreciation in the Manchurian Provinces and Hupei is equally marked. Many attempts have been made in different localities to regulate and maintain the specie value of the paper currency, but, as usual, these attempts have been futile. The redemption of these provincial paper notes by an issue of uniform convertible banknote currency is now being considered. TheShanghai *Shen Pao,* gives the following figures purporting to be authoritative:

Anhwei	$300,000	Kuangtung	$22,000,000
Chekiang	2,438,000	Kirin	14,456,000
Chihli	6,000	Kuangsi	2,186,000
Fuchien	300,000	Kweichow	1,768,000
Heilungkiang	2,518,000	Fengtien	5,184,000
Honan	1,482,000	Sinkiang	2,776,000
Hunan	10,570,000	Shantung	480,000
Hupei	30,000,000	Shansi	2,076,000
Jehol	14,000	Shensi	1,500,000
Kansu	282,000	Szechuan	11,592,000
Kiangsi	14,694,000	Yunnan	2,000,000
Kiangsu	1,124,000		
		Total	$129,746,000

Dr. Vissering, the monetary advisor, assisted by Dr. Roest, acting as his secretary, made an investigation into the currency conditions subsequent to his appointment, and the results of his investigations were embodied in a currency reform plan which he submitted to the Government late in 1912. Dr. Vissering's views and arguments may be briefly summarized:[2]

Dr. Vissering has reached the conclusion that the gold-exchange standard is the only feasible system for China and must be the goal of the currency reform. But he recog-

[1] *N. C. D. News,* Dec. 13, 1913.

[2] Dr. G. Vissering, *On Chinese Currency,* 1912.

nizes the complications created by the token money in introducing this system in a country with such enormous extent of territory and such divergent conditions and interests. He holds that "a token coin can only be issued by a Government which is powerful enough to prevent a serious degree of counterfeiting even in the remote interior and at the same time defend its frontiers against the importation of counterfeit money from abroad." Should the Government fail in either of these respects, the introduction of the gold-exchange standard would be an absolute failure, and the worst consequences would be experienced if the value of the token money could not be maintained. To avoid the necessity of introducing the token coins at the very beginning, Dr. Vissering suggests as a practical expedient, *a double standard*—not bimetallism, but two independent standards—a gold-exchange standard in co-existence with the present practically silver standard, the former gradually to supplant the latter during the period of transition, which the plan provides for.

This plan is based on the experiences of the Dutch East Indies and can be carried into effect without any serious difficulties. The first step to be taken for the practical execution of this plan would be for the Government to adopt at the outset a theoretical or bank unit with a fixed value in gold. The central Bank of Issue, which must be strengthened and operated on sound principles, may, as the next step in advance, issue notes on the gold basis, redeemable in gold values abroad, on presentation of sums amounting to 50,000 units and upwards. The foreign gold reserve, built up by the equivalent received against the issue of these notes, must be used for no other purpose than the maintenance of the values of these notes. As soon as possible, at least part of the reserve must be brought back to China. The great advantage of adopting the fictitious unit, according to Dr. Vissering, would be the certainty about the figure at which the future real gold unit will be adopted, thus preventing the speculation on the gold par and on the value of silver. There is no risk in following this course of action, and every step in the extension of this fictitious gold unit is so much advantage gained. During this stage, Dr. Vissering says, a study may be made of the actual conditions in regard to the balance of trade and of payment.

The next period in the reform of the currency begins with the issue of the token silver coins, and this can be begun as soon as the Government is strong enough to maintain the gold value of these coins. For the coinage ratio Dr. Vissering suggests a gold ratio of 21 to 1, which is approximately the same as the rupee, the yen and the Philippine dollar. The silver coin, provided for by the Act of May, 1911, the yuan of 72/100 K'up'ing tael, is considered too large, and a coin one-third of the K'up'ing tael is recommended. Taken at 28*d*. per oz. standard (444 grains fine) the equivalent of one-third K'up'ing tael (575.8 grains, 987 fine, or at 1000 fine, 568.3146 grains) would contain 189.4382 grains of fine silver: the gold value of the unit expressed in silver at the price of 28*d*. per oz. would be 11.946553*d*. The gold sovereign contains 7.32238 grams of fine gold. The proposed unit will have a gold value of 0.3644883 grams of fine gold:—7.322238 ÷ 240 × 11.946553. At the ratio of 21 to 1 the silver unit would contain 7.6542543 grams of fine silver, or a gross weight of 8.504727 grams, 900 fine. The subsidiary coins should have more alloy. Gold coins of 10 and 20 units may ultimately be coined, the former of the weight of 3.644883 grams fine gold and the latter of 7.289766 grams.

The withdrawal of the old silver and copper coins is the third and final stage of the reform. He suggests that Amsterdam, on account of its favorable location from a political point of view, may be selected for the location of the gold reserve that is to be kept abroad.

It may be well to give Dr. Vissering's outline of the proposed progress of the currency reform, as submitted to the Republican Government for its consideration.

First Period

1. The very first step must be the adoption of a future gold unit as a foundation of the new system, in order to avoid speculation on the announcement of the gold par, and also to avoid having at a later stage to raise the new unit to its future nominal value.

2. The organization of a central bank of issue, or otherwise the reorganization of the Ta Ch'ing Bank as a central bank for the whole country.

3. The introduction of the new gold unit as a money of account for book credits and book transfers.

4. Securing the co-operation of the foreign exchange banks and of the private Chinese banks and bankers for the introduction of the new gold unit into their bookkeeping.

5. The issue of banknotes based upon the new gold unit.

6. The accumulation of a gold reserve against the aforesaid banknotes.

7. The regulation of the management of this gold reserve.

8. Eventually declaring the banknotes legal tender.

9. To make a close study of the conditions of the balance of trade and of the balance of payment for China.

Second Period

10. The establishment of the weight, fineness and alloy of the token coins and of the new subsidiary coinage, by preference in the manner mentioned on page 136.

11. The issue of these token coins and subsidiary coins simultaneously.

12. The accumulation of a gold reserve against the token coins and the regulation of its management.

13. If desirable: the coinage and issue of gold coins, by preference in the manner mentioned on page 136. Also, if desirable, the temporary admission of some particular foreign gold coins as legal tender, and the temporary issue of gold certificates.

14. The proclamation as unlimited legal tender of:
   a. the silver token coins of 1 unit and 2 units;
   b. the above-mentioned gold coins and eventually the gold certificates.

Third Period

15. The gradual withdrawal and subsequent demonetization of the old silver dollars, as far as necessary of the old sycee, and of the present copper cash.

The Government, however, has no desire to undertake the task of introducing the gold standard and, at the time of this writing, has just announced its decision of introducing the national coinage on the basis of the silver standard. The National Coinage Act was promulgated by a Presidential Mandate on February 27, 1914, and the text was published in the leading dailies of the country. An English version of the text of the Act is given below. In many respects and in general principles the Act resembles the Act of May 24, 1910. But there are several provisions in the new Act that are improvements upon the old. There is an Article (Art. 12) providing for free coinage of the standard pieces, subject to a charge of 6/1000 of a K'up'ing tael. In other words, for the yuan of 648/1000 of a K'up'ing tael 1000 fine the Government will charge 654/1000 of a K'up'ing tael pure silver. This charge is made on the ground that, besides lessening the expenses of the reform, it will likewise prevent melting down the coins. This must be regarded as a sound policy.

Equally sound is the provision for coining the subsidiary

pieces at a much lower degree of fineness, whereby the expenses of recoining these minor pieces can be met when the system is put on the gold standard in the future. The proposed method of dealing with the old coins is that for the standard pieces the Government will give the new coins in exchange without charge, and that the subsidiary coins will be redeemed at their actual values according to the local market conditions. Within a prescribed period of time the old coins are to be permitted to circulate at a fixed value in the new coins and, in the case of the depreciated subsidiary coins, it is decided that the average value of the preceding month must be taken in the payment of public dues. The withdrawal of the old coins is the most difficult part of the reform, and would require most careful and intelligent handling. On this point perhaps too much stress cannot be laid.

The following is the text of the Act:

The New National Coinage Act promulgated by Presidential Mandate [1]

1. The right to coin and issue money shall belong exclusively to the Government.

2. The standard coin shall contain 648/1000 of a K'up'ing tael pure silver (23.97795048 grams) and shall be called yuan.

3. The different coins shall be as follows:

Silver coins: 1-yuan; half-yuan or 5-chiao; 2-chiao; 1-chiao.
Nickel coins: 5-fen.
Copper coins: 2-fen; 1-fen; 5-li; 2-li; 1-li.

4. The national coinage shall be on the decimal basis. The one-tenth of one yuan shall be one chiao; the one-hundredth of one yuan, one fen; the one-thousandth of one yuan, one li. All exchanges, public or private, must be at this rate.

[1] From *Shih Pao*, or Shanghai *Eastern Times*, translated by the author.

5. The weight and fineness of the different coins shall be as follows:

	Gross weight	Fineness
The standard coin yuan	$\frac{72}{100}$ of a K'up'ing tael	90% silver, 10% copper.
Half-yuan, or 5-chiao	$\frac{36}{100}$ " "	70% silver, 30% copper.
2-chiao	$\frac{144}{1000}$ " "	70% silver, 30% copper.
1-chiao	$\frac{72}{1000}$ " "	70% silver, 30% copper.
5-fen	$\frac{7}{100}$ " "	25% nickel, 75% copper.
2-fen	$\frac{28}{100}$ " "	95% copper, 4% zinc, 1% lead.
1-fen	$\frac{18}{100}$ " "	" " "
5-li	$\frac{9}{100}$ " "	" " "
2-li	$\frac{45}{1000}$ " "	" " "
1-li	$\frac{25}{1000}$ " "	" " "

6. There shall be no limitation upon the use of the standard coin. The 5-chiao coins may not be offered in excess of 20 yuan in any one payment. The 2-chiao and 1-chiao coins may not be offered in excess of 5 yuan in any one payment. The nickel and copper subsidiary coins may not be offered in excess of 1 yuan in any one payment. These limitations do not apply to the Government Bank in the exchange of coins or the Government offices in the payment of public dues.

7. The exact forms of the different coins will be determined by subsequent Presidential Mandate.

8. No coin of any denomination may differ from the legal weight by more than 3/1000. 1000 coins weighed together must not differ by more than 3/10,000 from the legal weight.

9. The fineness of the different silver coins must not differ from the legal standard by more than 3/1000.

10. When the standard coin has been so abraded by circulation and use that its weight has fallen by 1 per cent, and when the subsidiary coins, whether of silver, nickel, or copper, of 5-chiao and under, have lost by abrasion 5 per cent of their legal weight, they may be taken to the Government offices to be exchanged for new coins.

11. No one shall be compelled to accept mutilated coins when the mutilation can be shown to be intentional.

12. When silver bullion is presented by indivduals for coinage at the mints the Government must consent to give coins at a charge of 6/1000 of a K'up'ing tael a piece.

13. The date when this Act shall be effective will be determined by Presidential Mandate.

Mr. Liang C'hi-ch'ao, until lately Minister of Justice, has been appointed Director-General of the Currency Department. For the first time a competent single official has been put in charge of the execution of the reform, in place of the usual Commissions and Boards, and sometimes the entire Government. On account of this divided responsibility reform often ended with the drafting of the program. In all probability the reform will be launched as soon as political conditions become fairly settled, and enough funds are obtained. The Ministry of Finance has lately been negotiating to this end.

APPENDIX II

THE REGULATIONS OF NOVEMBER 19, 1905[1]

1. THE new silver currency should be purer in quality than the dollars heretofor coined in various provinces and the standard unit of value must be heavier to be suitable as a national coin. The purest silver in circulation in China to-day is shown by chemical analysis to contain not more than 98 or 99 per cent of pure silver, but a deduction of two or three per cent should be allowed in minting the new coin to cover the cost of coinage, and it is proposed to make the new tael of nine mace six candareens of pure silver, mixed with one mace's weight of pure copper, to be fixed as the equivalent of one K'up'ing tael of full touch.

The fractional currency shall consist (a) of a piece containing four mace eight candareens' weight of K'up'ing silver mixed with five candareens' weight of pure copper which shall be declared the equivalent of five mace K'up'ing silver full touch; (b) a piece of one mace seven candareens' weight of K'up'ing silver mixed with three candareens of pure copper, to be the equivalent of two mace K'up'ing silver of full touch; and (c) a piece of the weight of eight candareens five li of pure K'up'ing silver mixed with one candareen five li of pure copper, as the smallest piece, to be the equivalent of one mace of K'up'ing silver, full touch. It is also decided that in every ten pieces minted four shall

[1] In the *Report of the Director of the Mint of the U. S.*, 1906, pp. 198-200. Translation made by Mr. E. T. Williams, of the American Legation, Peking.

be of one tael's value and two of the denomination of five mace, two of two mace and two of one mace. This shall be the rule, but, if there shall be a demand for a larger proportion of any particular denomination, orders shall be issued to make a careful investigation as to the real amount (in circulation) and report upon the matter to the Financial Commission and the Board of Revenue, who shall consult together and make reply, and only if they consent may the additional amount be minted. As to these coins the central and branch mints must make them exactly of the same weight and fineness, and assay and inspection must be made according to the rules for the regulation of the coinage already submitted by us and approved by the Throne.

2. The 1-tael coin shall be equal to two 5-mace coins or five 2-mace coins, or ten 1-mace coins. The small fractional coins of less than five mace shall exchange among themselves at this rate, and in all monetary transactions, public or private, they must be paid out and received at this rate; under no circumstances may a discount be charged. Any disobedience will be punished according to law.

3. The 1-tael coin being the standard monetary unit, there shall be no limit to its circulation. The 5-mace and other fractional silver pieces shall be legal tender in every transaction to the amount of ten taels, *i. e.*, to the value of ten of the 1-tael coins. They must not be used to pay in full amounts over ten taels, and if offered they may be refused in amounts over the sum specified. The rate of exchange between the copper coins and the silver and the limit of circulation of the former will be determined after the provincial authorities have complied with the regulations already submitted, by which they are required to investigate and report to the Board of Revenue the facts as to the circulation of copper coins.

4. As to the minting of the silver coins, it is proposed

that, the Board of Revenue having been ordered to coin, the central mint will coin several million pieces and send them to the bank, and the Board of Revenue shall send dies to the provincial mints of Chili, Kiangsu, Hupeh and Kuangtung, which shall at the same time mint several million pieces, whereupon the bank of the Board of Revenue shall print paper money to the full amount of the silver coins minted and fix a date upon which it shall be put into circulation. After its issue the Treasury of the Board of Revenue and the treasuries of the provinces mentioned shall first receive it in a fixed proportion, and thereafter all the provinces, the railways, the (China Merchants) Steamship Company, and the Telegraph Administration shall receive it in the same proportion. There must be no discrimination against it by the said official companies on the ground that it is not issued in their provinces. The method of arranging the proportions shall be to fix the proportion payable in silver coins and that payable in paper money of the bank of the Board of Revenue, and for the present the remainder may be paid in other silver—that is, in lump silver or the old dollars—but afterwards as the coinage of the new pieces increases in amount the proportion payable in this may be increased until finally payments will be made entirely in the new silver coins. We request that orders be issued to all the Tartar generals, viceroys, and governors, as well as to the superintendent of railways, of the China Merchants Steam Navigation Company, and the Telegraph Administration to comply with this regulation.

5. All provincial taxes levied in K'up'ing taels shall be payable in the same amount of the new tael coins. The collectors should have salaries definitely fixed, *i. e.*, not be allowed to make their living by charges for exchange, *etc.*, as heretofore. Aside from the legal charge of meltage, no other charge shall be added to the sum levied under the

name of "assaying charges," *etc.* All other moneys heretofore collected or paid in taels of another scale shall be converted, according to the value of the tael used, into their equivalent in K'up'ing taels of full touch, and the conversion having once been made, these sums shall forever hereafter be receivable and payable in that amount of the new 1-tael coins, and no variation from the rule will be allowed. We have also to request that orders be issued to all the provincial authorities to comply with this rule.

6. As China is now entering into new commercial treaties with the various foreign powers which provide for the adoption of a uniform national coinage which the merchants of foreign nationalities residing in China shall use, it becomes necessary to request that the Board of Foreign Affairs be instructed that at the time of the issue of the new coinage dispatches must be sent to the various foreign ministers and to the consuls at the various treaty ports and notifications made to the commissioners of customs that they may all hereafter uniformly use the new coins. The customs duties have heretofore been levied and collected in Haikwan taels, and orders must be issued to the commissioners of customs thereafter in accordance with the provisions of the commercial treaties to convert the duties levied in Haikwan taels into their equivalent in K'up'ing taels and collect accordingly.

7. On the day when the new coins are put into circulation the viceroys and governors of the various provinces must issue instructions to the local authorities to put out proclamations informing the merchants and all people that whatever accounts they may have, old or new, and whatever commercial transactions may take place in the markets, the original amounts, according to the value of the taels in which they may be reckoned, must be converted to their equivalents in K'up'ing taels of full touch, and paid in that

amount of the new silver coins, and such payment may not be refused.

8. As all viceroys, governors, other officials, merchants, soldiers and common people in all the provinces must use the new coins, all may send their silver to be minted, and the central mint and the branch mints at Tientsin, Nanking, Wuchang and Canton will coin it for them. Every tael of K'up'ing silver of full touch will be refined to pure silver 0.985 fine, or finer, in return for which (0.985 tael) they will receive one of the new tael dollars. Fractional coins of the denomination of five mace, two mace, and one mace will also be minted for them in the proportions set forth above.

The excess in the fineness of the silver will pay the cost of minting, and thus there will be nothing to make good on either side.

Silver of inferior quality, foreign silver coins, and the silver dollars heretofore minted in the various provinces may also be sent in to be reminted, the amount of the new coins given in exchange being determined by the amount of pure silver contained—that is, their value will be determined in K'up'ing taels of full touch, and new coins issued accordingly.

9. When the new coins are first issued and the people are unfamiliar with them, there will almost surely be attempts made among the merchants in exchanging them to discriminate against them (boycott them), or to discount them. The Bank of the Board of Revenue, the customs banks in the various provinces, and other official banks and cash shops must be charged with the responsibility of seeing that any one bringing the new silver coins to exchange for paper money, bullion, or copper coins, or desiring to exchange paper money, silver bullion, or copper coins for the new silver coins, shall receive just treatment

on the basis of one K'up'ing tael being the equivalent of one tael in the new coinage. There must be no extortion. Orders must be given also to investigate the markets, and if any mercantile firms are found raising or lowering the rate of exchange at their own pleasure, report shall be made for cases in Peking to the Financial Commission and to the Board of Revenue, and for the provinces to the Tartar generals, viceroys, and the governors concerned, who shall investigate and severely punish the offence, so as to enforce the coinage regulations.

10. These regulations must be published in the official gazettes for the information of the people, and we have to request that orders be issued to the Tartar generals, viceroys and governors of the various provinces that at the time when the new coins are issued they must instruct the department and district magistrates to print these regulations in large characters in proclamations which must be posted in all the cities, villages, and market towns of their jurisdictions, that the people on seeing the same may become thoroughly acquainted with the matter, and thus the yamen clerks may be kept from cheating them.

APPENDIX III

Regulations for the National Coinage of May 24, 1910[1] (with Original Explanatory Notes)

Article 1. The monetary unit of the Ta Ch'ing Empire shall be called the dollar (yuan).[2]

Art. 2. The different coins shall be as follows:

Silver coins: (1) One-dollar coins; (2) fifty-cent coins; (3) twenty-five cent coins; (4) ten-cent coins.

Nickel coins: (1) Five-cent coins.

The coinage of this nickel coin will be delayed pending an investigation into mines and methods of mintage.

Copper coins: (1) Two-cent coins; (2) one-cent coins; (3) five-mill coins; (4) one-mill coins.

The coinage of the one-cent copper coins will be postponed, owing to the danger of their being confounded with the ten-cash coins formerly minted.

Art. 3. The dollar (yuan) will be the standard coin, and the coins from the fifty cents and under will be considered subsidiary coinage, and will be in the decimal system. One dollar will be ten dimes. One dime will be ten cents. One cent will be ten mills. All exchanges must be at this rate.

Art. 4. The weight and fineness of the silver coins will be as follows: The weight of one dollar will be seventy-two

[1] In *U. S. Mint Report*, 1911, pp. 236-8. Translation by Dr. C. D. Tenney, of the American Legation, Peking.

[2] The monetary unit means that used in computations above unity. Below unity the reckoning is decimal.

hundredths of a K'up ing tael, and the fineness ninety per cent, amounting to six hundred and forty-eight thousandths of a tael of silver.

The weight of the fifty-cent pieces will be thirty-six hundredths of a K'up'ing tael and eighty per cent fineness, amounting to two hundred and eighty-eight thousandths of a tael of silver.

The weight of the twenty-five cent piece will be eighteen hundredths of a K'up'ing tael, and the fineness eighty per cent, amounting to one hundred and forty-four thousandths of a tael of silver.

The weight of the ten-cent piece will be 864/10000 of a K'up'ing tael, and the fineness sixty-five per cent, so containing 5616/100000 of a tael of silver.

The weight and fineness of the nickel and copper coins will be determined later.[1]

Art. 5. There will no limitation in the use of the standard dollar.

The subsidiary silver coins may not be offered in excess of five dollars' worth in any one payment. The nickel and copper subsidiary coins may not be offered in excess of half a dollar's worth in any one payment.

Payment of the subsidiary coins in excess of the above amounts may be refused, but this does not apply to the Ta Ch'ing Bank or any of its branches in the exchange of coins.[2]

[1] In these regulations the "K'u-p'ing tael" refers to the K'u-p'ing tael as determined in response to the joint memorial of the Board of Agriculture, Industry, and Commerce, and the Board of Finance in regard to uniform weights and measures. Therein it was specified that the K'u-p'ing tael would be reckoned as equivalent to thirty-seven and three hundred and one one-thousandths (37.301) grams by the French metric system. The silver referred to is to be absolutely pure silver.

[2] Therefore in all financial operations the dollar will be current,

Art. 6. On one face of the silver dollar will be a dragon and on the other face the characters "Ta Ch'ing Silver Coin, One Dollar." The subsidiary coins of silver, nickel, and copper will be minted on the same general model.[1]

Art. 7. No dollar may differ from the legal weight by more than two one-thousandths of a K'up'ing tael. One thousand coins weighed together must not differ more than three one-thousandths of the legal weight.[2]

Art. 8. The fineness of silver coins must not differ from the legal standard more than three one-thousandths.[3]

Art. 9. When a dollar coin has been so abraded by use that its weight has fallen below seventy-one one-hundredths tael, and when the fractional coins, whether of silver, nickel, or copper, of fifty cents and under, show signs of

whether the transactions are in tens, hundreds, thousands, or tens of thousands. The purpose in minting the subsidiary coins is to provide for small transactions in trade and for reckoning change; so the limit for the use of them must be clearly defined. But exchanging coins and using them are different, and therefore there is no limit in matters of exchange. So the subsidiary coinage is protected and the people's confidence in it will not be impaired. If it be found that the absence of a limitation in the matter of exchanging coins will lead to the banks receiving large amounts of the subsidiary coins so that they cannot avoid offering temptation to counterfeiters, it should be remembered that there is a fixed limit to the number of subsidiary coins that may be minted and those who care to exchange them will naturally be few. Also there is a regular medium of exchange so that the counterfeiting may be easily discovered. So no fear need be entertained on this score.

[1] The exact forms of the silver, nickel, and copper coins will be sent to all the Provinces.

[2] In enforcing the first and second parts of this article some liberality may be shown in reckoning and passing single silver dollars, but the reckoning by thousands will be strictly observed.

[3] Differences in weight in numbers of coins will be determined according to the provisions of the last Article, but differences in fineness according to this Article.

abrasion, they may be taken to the mint or to the Ta Ch'ing Bank to be exchanged for new coins.[1]

Art. 10. No one can be compelled to accept mutilated coins, when the mutilation can be shown to be intentional.[2]

Art. 11. The Board of Finance will fix the limit for the amount of coinage of the subsidiary coins.[3]

Supplementary Articles

Art. 12. The Ta Ch'ing Bank will appoint a special official to control carefully all matters connected with the exchanging of coins, both old and new.[4]

Art. 13. During the introductory period of issuing the new coins, one dollar and fifty cents will be reckoned as one tael of the Board of Finance Treasury weight, standard silver.[5]

Art. 14. In places where the new coins have been issued, the large and small coins previously minted may continue to circulate temporarily at their market value. On the one hand, the Government mints and the Ta Ch'ing Bank will

[1] Silver coins used in trade cannot fail to be abraded, therefore the limit of seventy-one one-hundredths teal will be set for abrasion. When this limit of abrasion is exceeded the coins must be exchanged to secure confidence.

[2] The last Article provides for the exchange of coins abraded by use, and this Article forbids the exchange of coins deliberately mutilated, in order to prevent the people from boring holes, affixing stamps, or grinding off the coins.

[3] The coinage of the subsidiary coins must be limited, and they must not be issued in excessive quantities to avoid injuring their currency as subsidiary coins.

[4] The exchanging of the old and new coins is the special business of the bank, but since the business of the bank is complicated, a special bank officer will be deputed to control this department so that it may be properly managed.

[5] This Article fixes the exchange value of the new and old money and the standard for discounting. By standard silver is meant silver of nine hundred and eighty-five one-thousandths fineness.

gradually withdraw them at the market rate to be reminted into the new coinage; and on the other hand, the Board of Finance will take all the circumstances into consideration, and fix a limit of time for this to continue. After the time fixed, all such circulation will cease, and the mints and the Ta Ch'ing Bank will exchange the old coins as silver bullion.

Art. 15. The copper coins previously minted in the Provinces will continue to circulate at their market value and the Board of Finance will regulate this matter in accordance with circumstances.[1]

Art. 16. After the regulations have been approved by imperial rescript, a limit of one year will be granted within which period all regular official receipts and disbursements will be converted into Treasury taels of standard silver and then reckoned in the new monetary unit.[2]

Art. 17. A limit of one year will be fixed after the date of the imperial sanction of these regulations, and within this time all official receipts and disbursements regularly made in copper cash or silver shall be reckoned in Treasury

[1] In regard to the method of treating the old coinage as laid down in Articles 14 and 15, the Board of Finance will determine a special method of treatment after considering the conditions and will memorialize the throne on the subject.

[2] In order to unify the currency system ail accounts and public documents will first use the new monetary denominations. This is to hasten the adoption of the new monetary unit, and the resulting advantages in making and auditing the budgets will be many. Therefore before the new coins have been issued there is no difficulty about fixing a limit of time within which the new terminology shall replace the old. So if the former reckoning in taels is changed to dollars it will not be troublesome to use the ratio of exchange laid down in Article 13. Therefore fixing a year as the limit for the change is not too rapid. If it is found that the new coins will not be immediately sufficient for use till after the change of name, the silver bullion and old coins may continue to be used and the actual receipts and disbursements may be reckoned in Treasury taels of standard silver and then reckoned in the national coin. This will cause no inconvenience.

taels and thence converted into national dollars. In cases where silver dollars or other coins have hitherto been used, the same method shall be followed.[1]

Art. 18. All customs, postal, telegraph, steamer, and railway accounts shall be tendered in the national coinage after being first changed into Treasury taels by the heads of the offices concerned according to the weights and purity of the money received or disbursed, within one year of the time when these regulations receive the imperial sanction.[2]

Art. 19. All debts of the common people which are reckoned in silver shall be reckoned in Treasury taels according to the weight and fineness of silver in the locality concerned and then reckoned in the national coinage. When they are reckoned in the old silver dollars, copper-minted coins, copper cash, or any other kind of money they shall be reckoned in Treasury taels according to the market rate for the place, fixed by decree on memorial as provided in these regulations, and then reckoned in the national coinage. In all cases, in which the documents have not been reckoned in the national coinage, as laid down in this Article, if there shall be any litigation, judgment shall be given according to the rate for the day fixed by edict, on memorial, as prescribed in these regulations.[3]

[1] In changing the unit of reckoning according to this Article, public accounts and documents shall be first changed and the market rate for the day fixed by the throne, on memorial, shall be used in order to prevent brokers from lowering or raising the exchange and to avoid dispute about exchange. The method of carrying out this provision shall be for the Board of Finance to telegraph to every Province, obtaining the market rates for all sorts of silver money in every *fu*, *ting*, *chou*, and *hsien*, which the Board will publish in every locality.

[2] Since the large customs accounts and the communication accounts have an important influence upon currency, they should be first changed so as to promote the use of the new currency.

[3] The different kinds of money alluded to in this Article and Article 17 are the Tientsin "ching ch'ien," Hsinchiang "hung ch'ien," and other such coins.

Art. 20. From the date when these regulations receive the imperial sanction, all mintage of large and small silver and copper coins in the Provinces shall cease.

Art. 21. The Board of Finance will establish an assay office and engage an expert to take charge of it. Specimen coins will be taken from the coins minted by the mints, which shall be assayed and the analysis will be published.[1]

Art. 22. Throughout the Ta Ch'ing Empire when the Ta Ch'ing national coins are offered in payment, no matter who the person may be or what the account may be, the national money may not be refused.[2]

Art. 23. Any one who violates the provisions of Article 3 or Article 22 may be accused in court by the person concerned. After conviction a fine of from $10 to $1,000 will be inflicted.[3]

Art. 24. If these regulations require alteration, the Board of Finance will memorialize the Throne publicly thereon.

[1] The coins selected will be either from those already in circulation or from those just minted, and the analysis will be for the purpose of maintaining confidence.

[2] This article defines the legal-tender quality of the national coins, and is in accordance with the regulations of all countries.

[3] Violating Article 3 means forcing one to discount coins, so interfering with the decimal value of the subsidiary coins. Violating Article 22 means that when the national currency is offered one refuses to accept it.

APPENDIX IV

Gold Price of Bar Silver

HIGHEST, LOWEST, AND AVERAGE PRICE OF BAR SILVER IN LONDON, PER OUNCE BRITISH STANDARD (0.925), AND THE EQUIVALENT IN U. S. GOLD COIN OF AN OUNCE 1000 FINE, TAKEN AT THE AVERAGE PRICE, SINCE 1871

	Highest quotation	Lowest quotation	Average quotation	Value of a fine ounce at average quotation
	d.	*d.*	*d.*	
1871	61	60 3/16	60½	$1.326
1872	62⅛	59¼	60 5/16	1.322
1873	59 15/16	57⅞	59 3/16	1.29769
1874	59½	57¼	58 5/16	1.27883
1875	57⅝	55½	56 11/16	1.24233
1876	58½	46¾	53⅛	1.16414
1877	58¼	53¼	54 13/16	1.20189
1878	55¼	49½	52⅝	1.15358
1879	53¾	48⅞	51¼	1.12392
1880	52 13/16	51½	52¼	1.14507
1881	52⅞	50⅞	51⅝	1.13229
1882	52⅜	50	51 13/16	1.13562
1883	51 3/16	50 1/16	50 9/16	1.10874
1884	51⅜	49½	50 11/16	1.11068
1885	50	46⅞	48 9/16	1.06510
1886	47	42	45⅜	.99467
1887	47⅛	43¼	44 11/16	.97946
1888	44 9/16	41⅝	42⅞	.93974
1889	44⅜	41 15/16	42 11/16	.93511
1890	54⅝	43⅝	47¾	1.04634
1891	48¾	43½	45 1/16	.98800
1892	43¾	37⅞	39¾	.87145
1893	38¾	30½	35 9/16	.78030
1894	31¾	27	28 15/16	.63479
1895	31⅜	27 3/16	29 13/16	.65406
1896	31 15/16	29¾	30 13/16	.67565
1897	29 13/16	23⅝	27 9/16	.60438
1898	28⅜	25	26 15/16	.59010
1899	29	26⅝	27 7/16	.60154

	Highest quotation	Lowest quotation	Average quotation	Value of a fine ounce at average quotation
	d.	*d.*	*d.*	
1900	30¼	27	28 5/16	.62007
1901	29 9/16	24 15/16	27 3/16	.59595
1902	26 1/16	21 11/16	24 1/16	.52795
1903	28½	21 11/16	24¾	.54257
1904	28 9/16	24 7/16	26 13/32	.57876
1905	30 5/16	25 7/16	27 13/16	.61027
1906	33⅛	29	30⅞	.67689
1907	37 7/16	24¼	30 3/16	.66152
1908	27	22	24 13/32	.53490
1909	24⅞	23 1/16	23 23/32	.52016
1910	26¼	23 3/16	24 21/32	.54077
1911			24.592	.53304
1912			28.842	.60835
1913			27.576	.59791

VITA

The author was born in Mi-yun Hsien near Peking, China, August 1, 1888. He was prepared for college in the Peking University Preparatory College and attended the College of Liberal Arts of that institution, from which he graduated with the A. B. degree in 1908. He passed the Government competitive examination, was granted a scholarship and came to the United States in 1909. He studied at Amherst College during the years 1909-11, graduating *cum laude* with the A. B. degree in 1910 and receiving the A. M. degree in 1911. He entered the School of Political Science of Columbia University in the fall of 1911. At Columbia he studied under Professors Seligman, Seager, Clark, John B. Moore, Goodnow and Giddings, and attended the seminars of Professors Seligman and Seager.

Bei Fragen zur Produktsicherheit wenden Sie sich bitte an:
If you have any questions regarding product safety,
please contact:

Walter de Gruyter GmbH
Genthiner Straße 13
10785 Berlin
productsafety@degruyterbrill.com